CUPCAKES
AND MUFFINS

CUPCAKES
AND MUFFINS

IRRESISTIBLE CREATIONS FOR EVERY OCCASION:
150 DELICIOUS RECIPES SHOWN IN 300 STUNNING PHOTOGRAPHS

Carol Pastor

LORENZ BOOKS

This edition is published by Lorenz Books, an imprint of Anness Publishing Ltd, 108 Great Russell Street, London WC1B 3NA; info@anness.com

www.lorenzbooks.com; www.annesspublishing.com

If you like the images in this book and
would like to investigate using them for publishing, promotions or advertising, please visit our website www.practicalpictures.com for more information.

A CIP catalogue record for this book is available from the British Library.

Publisher: Joanna Lorenz
Editors: Amy Christian
Designer: Sarah Rock
Recipes: Carol Pastor
Photography: Charlie Richards and Craig Robertson
Stylists: Liz Hippisley and Helen Trent
Production Controller: Pirong Wang
Index: Ann Barrett

NOTES
Bracketed terms are intended for American readers.
For all recipes, quantities are given in both metric and imperial measures and, where appropriate, in standard cups and spoons. Follow one set of measures, but not a mixture, because they are not interchangeable.
Standard spoon and cup measures are level. 1 tsp = 5ml, 1 tbsp = 15ml, 1 cup = 250ml/8fl oz.
Australian standard tablespoons are 20ml. Australian readers should use 3 tsp in place of 1 tbsp for measuring small quantities.
American pints are 16fl oz/2 cups. American readers should use 20fl oz/ 2.5 cups in place of 1 pint when measuring liquids.
Electric oven temperatures in this book are for conventional ovens. When using a fan oven, the temperature will probably need to be reduced by about 10–20°C/20–40°F. Since ovens vary, you should check with your manufacturer's instruction book for guidance.
The nutritional analysis given for each recipe is calculated per portion (i.e. serving or item), unless otherwise stated. If the recipe gives a range, such as Serves 4–6, then the nutritional analysis will be for the smaller portion size, i.e. 6 servings. The analysis does not include optional ingredients, such as salt added to taste.
Medium (US large) eggs are used unless otherwise stated.

Front cover shows Madeleine Cakes with Raspberry Buttercream – for recipe see page 131.

Contents

Introduction

Equally delicious, freshly baked cupcakes and muffins are always a treat to be enjoyed. With recipes for breakfast muffins, savoury muffins, classic teatime treats, fruity bakes, sweet and indulgent cakes and ideas for special occasions, there is something for everyone.

The way that cupcakes and muffins are baked – in a muffin tin (pan) lined with paper cases – gives them a similar appearance, but there are some differences. A cupcake is baked with flour and is almost always sweet with a characteristic decorative frosting. Muffins can be sweet, often with a fruit flavouring, but can also be savoury, and are often eaten for breakfast. In its early form, a muffin would have been made with different grains, giving it a heavier texture. The 'muffin method' of baking is quite different to the cupcake. Muffins are made in two stages: the dry ingredients (flour, sugar, dried fruit, nuts and so on) are mixed together in one bowl and the wet (eggs, oil or melted butter) in another. The two are mixed together just enough to dampen the flour with as few strokes as possible.

CUPCAKES

First made during the Victorian period, cupcakes were originally made using a classic Victoria sponge recipe with simple decorations such as angelica or candied fruit. These light confections were named fairy cakes in Britain and were enjoyed with afternoon tea. American cooks made them larger, used rich buttercream with blueberries or chocolate and named them cupcakes – possibly because the recipe for the sponge called for a cupful of each ingredient.

Today the names 'fairy cake' and 'cupcake' are almost interchangeable. They are a sweet cake that everyone recognizes and are guaranteed to evoke fond memories. These delightful cakes, each presented in individual portions, appeal to our sense of nostalgia. They represent comfort food, a sweet treat, and are often associated with memories of childhood attempts at home baking. Today these confections have caught the public imagination. Timeless recipes for vanilla, lemon, chocolate and cherry cakes have become the mainstay of tearooms and cafés everywhere, from country

BELOW: *Cupcakes are often decorated with coloured frosting and elegant motifs, such as flowers pressed out of sugarpaste.*

ABOVE: *Savoury muffins, flavoured with cheese, herbs or spices, are perfect served with a warming soup.*

ABOVE: *Even the simplest sponge cupcakes can be made to look spectacular with a few carefully chosen sprinkles.*

ABOVE: *A batch of muffins can be baked in different-shaped pans, or even mini flowerpots, for an interesting effect.*

tea gardens to über-trendy city patisseries. They are the perfect recipe to serve for afternoon tea, to dress up with fruit and ice cream as a divine dessert, and to fill with mouthfuls of indulgent creamy icing. They have become, too, a common centrepiece for christenings and anniversaries.

MUFFINS
Two types of muffin are popular today – the English muffin, an individual round, flat bread, made of dough, baked on a griddle, and often served toasted and spread with butter, and the American muffin, a little cake, usually sweet, baked in the oven. English and American muffins are distinct from each other in taste and texture, and apart from in name are unlikely ever to

be confused. American muffins originated as small baked breads, but with the introduction of new raising agents in the mid-19th century, and the addition of a wider range of ingredients in recent decades, they have evolved to become more cake-like. Baked in a muffin tin and with a distinct cup shape and golden domed top, the muffin can be filled with sweet or savoury ingredients, and have a light or dense texture.

Versatile and practical, there are muffins in this book to suit every occasion. They are perfect for breakfast when filled with nutritious oats and dried fruits, or for packing in a lunch box with an apple and a carton of fruit juice. Left plain, or drizzled with syrup, a fruit-packed muffin is a great

pick-me-up for any time of day. Mini muffins filled with vegetables make delightful savoury appetizers or accompaniments that are the perfect side dish to soups and salads.

ABOUT THIS BOOK
Whether you choose an indulgent chocolate cupcake or a classic blueberry muffin, an elegant vanilla butterfly cupcake or a savoury chilli cheese muffin, each is sure to be delicious. So if you are deciding what to bake for your next tea party, beach party, children's birthday, wedding breakfast or friends' reunion, or even if you just want something tasty to eat with a pot of tea at your own kitchen table with a friend, this book has plenty of simple, creative and elegant ideas.

Breakfast muffins

This delightful recipe collection is packed

with familiar breakfast fare – toasted oats

and bran, honey and marmalade, lightly

spiced fresh and dried fruits, and chopped

nuts and yogurt. With a pot of strong tea or

espresso coffee they make a ritual to savour.

Try Berry Brioche Muffins split open and

spread with butter and a spoonful of dark

berry preserve, or Spiced Sultana Muffins

full of dried fruits.

Honey and yogurt muffins

These filling and substantial wholemeal breakfast muffins are made with honey rather than with sugar, so are not overly sweet. Different flavours of honey will give a subtle changes in taste.

MAKES 12

55g/2oz/¼ cup butter
75ml/5 tbsp clear honey
250ml/8fl oz/1 cup natural
   (plain) yogurt
1 egg
grated rind of 1 lemon
65ml/2fl oz lemon juice
150g/5oz/1¼ cups plain
   (all-purpose) flour
175g/6oz/1½ cups wholemeal
   (whole-wheat) flour
7.5ml/1½ tsp bicarbonate of soda
   (baking soda)
pinch of freshly grated nutmeg

1 Preheat the oven to 190°C/375°F/Gas 5. Line the cups of a muffin tin (pan) with paper cases.

2 In a small pan, melt the butter and honey over a gentle heat. Stir to combine. Remove from the heat and set aside to cool slightly.

3 In a bowl, whisk together the yogurt, egg, lemon rind and juice. Add the butter and honey mixture. Set aside. In another bowl, sift together the dry ingredients. Fold the dry ingredients into the yogurt mixture to blend, then fill the prepared cups two-thirds full.

4 Bake until the tops spring back when touched lightly. This should be around 20 minutes. Leave to cool for 5 minutes before turning out on to a wire rack.

5 Serve the muffins warm, drizzled with honey, if you like.

Nutritional information per portion: Energy 155kcal/652kJ; Protein 4.7g; Carbohydrate 25.4g, of which sugars 6.9g; Fat 4.6g, of which saturates 2.5g; Cholesterol 25mg; Calcium 66mg; Fibre 1.7g; Sodium 50mg.

Oat and raisin muffins

Rolled oats are a versatile cereal with many health-giving benefits, more often associated with porridge at breakfast time. They help lower cholesterol and are full of dietary fibre.

MAKES 12

85g/3oz/generous 1 cup rolled oats
250ml/8fl oz/1 cup buttermilk
120g/4oz/½ cup butter, softened
100g/3½oz/scant ½ cup soft dark
    brown sugar
1 egg
115g/4oz/1 cup plain (all-purpose) flour
5ml/1 tsp baking powder
2.5ml/½ tsp bicarbonate of soda
    (baking soda)
30g/1oz/3 tbsp raisins

1 In a large bowl, combine the oats and buttermilk and leave to soak for about 1 hour.

2 Preheat the oven to 200°C/400°F/Gas 6. Lightly grease the cups of a muffin tin (pan) or line them with paper cases.

3 With an electric whisk, cream the butter and sugar until light and fluffy. Beat in the egg. Sift the flour, baking powder and bicarbonate of soda. Stir the flour mixture into the butter mixture.

4 Add the oat mixture, then fold in the raisins. Do not overmix.

5 Two-thirds fill each of the prepared cups. Bake in the oven for 20–25 minutes. Transfer to a wire rack to cool. Store the muffins in an airtight container for up to 3 days.

Nutritional information per portion: Energy 177kcal/742kJ; Protein 3g; Carbohydrate 22.3g, of which sugars 10.4g; Fat 9.1g, of which saturates 5.2g; Cholesterol 37mg; Calcium 51mg; Fibre 0.8g; Sodium 77mg.

Crunchy breakfast muffins

Toasted oat cereals are widely available and make a delicious and crunchy addition to these moreish muffins. The raisins add sweetness to the light texture of this batter. Serve with strong coffee for a late breakfast or brunch.

MAKES 10

150g/5oz/1¼ cups plain
   (all-purpose) flour
7.5ml/1½ tsp baking powder
30ml/2 tbsp caster (superfine) sugar
250ml/8fl oz/1 cup milk
1 egg
50g/2oz/¼ cup butter, melted
200g/7oz toasted oat cereal and raisins mixed

1 Preheat the oven to 350°F/180°C/Gas 4. Lightly grease the cups of a muffin tin (pan) or line them with paper cases.

2 Sift the flour into a bowl. Add the baking powder, then the sugar, and stir in. Make a well in the centre.

3 Pour the milk into a jug (pitcher), add the egg and the melted butter and, using a fork, beat together thoroughly.

4 Pour the liquid into the well in the flour mixture. Stir in lightly until the wet and dry ingredients are just combined.

5 Stir in the cereal and raisins. Fill the prepared cups two-thirds full. Bake for 20–22 minutes until risen and golden. Leave to cool in the tin for a few minutes, then turn out on to a wire rack to go completely cold. Serve fresh, or store in an airtight container for up to 3 days.

Nutritional information per portion: Energy 212kcal/878kJ; Protein 6.2g; Carbohydrate 5.5g, of which sugars 0.7g; Fat 18.6g, of which saturates 11.7g; Cholesterol 73mg; Calcium 125mg; Fibre 0.2g; Sodium 503mg.

Prune muffins

Sticky and full of flavour, the humble prune is low in fat, full of fibre and contains antioxidants and minerals in abundance, making it a healthy choice of dried fruit.

MAKES 12

1 egg
250ml/8fl oz/1 cup milk
120ml/4fl oz/½ cup vegetable oil
50g/2oz/4 tbsp caster
   (superfine) sugar
25g/1oz/2 tbsp soft dark brown sugar
285g/10oz/2½ cups plain
   (all-purpose) flour
10ml/2 tsp baking powder
pinch of grated nutmeg
115g/4oz cooked pitted
   prunes, chopped

1 Preheat the oven to 200°C/400°F/ Gas 6. Grease the cups of a muffin tin (pan) or line with paper cases.

2 Break the egg into a bowl and beat with a fork. Beat in the milk and oil. Stir in the sugars. Set aside.

3 Sift the flour, baking powder and nutmeg into a mixing bowl.

4 Make a well in the centre, pour in the egg mixture and stir until moistened. Do not overmix; the batter should be slightly lumpy.

5 Fold in the prunes. Fill the prepared cups two-thirds full. Bake until golden brown, about 20 minutes. Let stand for 10 minutes before turning out on to a wire rack.

Nutritional information per portion: Energy 190kcal/801kJ; Protein 3.7g; Carbohydrate 28.1g, of which sugars 10.7g; Fat 7.8g, of which saturates 1.2g; Cholesterol 17mg; Calcium 66mg; Fibre 1.3g; Sodium 17mg.

Raisin and bran muffins

Low in fat and sugar, these dense and filling muffins are made with a combination of wholemeal flour and bran, and are flavoured with cinnamon and raisins.

MAKES 5

40g/1½ oz/⅓ cup plain
  (all-purpose) flour
55g/2oz/½ cup wholemeal
  (whole-wheat) flour
7.5ml/1½ tsp bicarbonate of soda
  (baking soda)
5ml/1 tsp ground cinnamon
30g/1oz/⅓ cup bran
85g/3oz raisins
65g/2½oz/⅓ cup soft dark brown sugar
50g/2oz/¼ cup caster (superfine) sugar
1 egg, beaten
250ml/8fl oz/1 cup buttermilk
juice of ½ lemon
50g/2oz/¼ cup butter, melted

1 Preheat the oven to 200°C/400°F/ Gas 6. Grease the cups of a muffin tin (pan) or line them with paper cases.

2 In a bowl, sift together the flours, bicarbonate of soda and cinnamon. Add the bran, raisins and sugars and stir until blended.

3 In another bowl, mix together the egg, buttermilk, lemon juice and melted butter. Add the buttermilk mixture to the dry ingredients.

4 Whisk lightly and quickly until just moistened. Do not overmix.

5 Spoon the mixture into the prepared paper cases, filling the cups almost to the top. Half-fill any empty cups with water so that the muffins bake evenly.

6 Bake for 15–20 minutes. Let stand for 5 minutes, before turning out on to a wire rack. Serve warm or at room temperature.

Nutritional information per portion: Energy 89kcal/374kJ; Protein 2g; Carbohydrate 13.4g, of which sugars 8.9g; Fat 3.4g, of which saturates 1.9g; Cholesterol 20mg; Calcium 34mg; Fibre 1.1g; Sodium 36mg.

Apricot bran muffins

These fruity muffins, packed with dried apricots and bran, are more nutritious for breakfast than a slice of toast. Packed with iron, fibre and vitamin A, dried apricots are associated with many health-giving properties. Choose organic varieties for a deeper flavour.

MAKES 12

115g/4oz/½ cup dried apricots
225g/8oz/2 cups self-raising
   (self-rising) flour
50g/2oz/½ cup wheat or oat bran
2.5ml/½ tsp bicarbonate of soda (baking soda)
30ml/2 tbsp soft light brown sugar

30ml/2 tbsp butter, melted
150g/¼ pint/⅔ cup natural
   (plain) yogurt
200ml/7fl oz/scant 1 cup milk

1 Grease the cups of a muffin tin (pan) or line them with paper cases.

2 Soak the dried apricots in a small bowl of water for 15 minutes. Roughly chop the soaked apricots into small bitesize pieces.

3 Preheat the oven to 220°C/425°F/Gas 7.

4 In a large bowl, mix together the flour, bran, bicarbonate of soda, sugar and chopped apricots.

5 Add the melted butter, yogurt and milk to the bowl of dry ingredients. Mix lightly.

6 Two-thirds fill the prepared paper cases with batter. Bake for 15–20 minutes until a skewer inserted into the centre of one comes out clean.

7 Leave the muffins to set for 5 minutes, then turn out on to a wire rack to cool. Serve warm or eat within 2 days.

Nutritional information per portion: Energy 131kcal/553kJ; Protein 4g; Carbohydrate 23.6g, of which sugars 8.3g; Fat 3g, of which saturates 1.7g; Cholesterol 7mg; Calcium 83mg; Fibre 2.7g; Sodium 42mg.

Apple and cinnamon muffins

A classic and winning combination of ingredients, spiced apples have the most delicious aroma when they are baking. Eat these fruity muffins while they are still warm.

MAKES 6

1 egg, beaten
40g/1½oz/3 tbsp caster
    (superfine) sugar
120ml/4fl oz/½ cup milk
50g/2oz/¼ cup butter, melted
150g/5oz/1¼ cups plain
    (all-purpose) flour
7.5ml/1½ tsp baking powder
2.5ml/½ tsp ground cinnamon
2 small eating apples, peeled,
    cored and finely chopped

FOR THE TOPPING
12 brown sugar cubes, crushed
5ml/1 tsp ground cinnamon

1 Preheat the oven to 200°C/400°F/ Gas 6. Line the cups of a muffin tin (pan) with paper cases.

2 Mix the egg, sugar, milk and melted butter in a large bowl. Sift in the flour, baking powder and cinnamon.

3 Add the chopped apples and mix roughly. Spoon the mixture into the prepared paper cases.

4 To make the topping, mix the crushed sugar cubes with the cinnamon. Sprinkle over the batter.

5 Bake for 30–35 minutes, until well risen and golden. Leave to stand for 5 minutes before transferring to a wire rack to cool.

6 Serve the muffins warm or at room temperature. Store in an airtight container for up to 3 days.

Nutritional information per portion: Energy 236kcal/995kJ; Protein 4.3g; Carbohydrate 38.2g, of which sugars 19.1g; Fat 8.5g, of which saturates 4.9g; Cholesterol 51mg; Calcium 74mg; Fibre 1.2g; Sodium 73mg.

Cherry and marmalade muffins

Bursting with fruit and a sweet taste, these muffins are topped like toast, with marmalade. Choose quality brands for the best flavour, and try lime or lemon marmalade for a change.

MAKES 12

225g/8oz/2 cups self-raising (self-rising) flour
5ml/1 tsp mixed (apple pie) spice
85g/3oz/scant ½ cup caster (superfine) sugar
120g/4oz/½ cup glacé (candied) cherries, quartered
30ml/2 tbsp orange marmalade
150ml/¼ pint/⅔ cup milk
50g/2oz/4 tbsp butter, melted
marmalade, to glaze

1 Preheat the oven to 200°C/400°F/ Gas 6. Grease the cups of a muffin tin (pan) or line with paper cases.

2 Sift the flour into a bowl. Add the spice. Stir in the sugar and cherries.

3 Mix the marmalade with the milk in a jug (pitcher).

4 Fold the milk mixture into the dry ingredients with the butter.

5 Spoon into the paper cases. Bake for 20–25 minutes, until golden.

6 Turn out on to a wire rack and brush with warmed marmalade. Store in an airtight container for 3 days.

Nutritional information per portion: Energy 162kcal/686kJ; Protein 2.3g; Carbohydrate 29.8g, of which sugars 15.5g; Fat 4.6g, of which saturates 0.7g; Cholesterol 1mg; Calcium 51mg; Fibre 0.7g; Sodium 9mg.

Banana and raisin muffins

Sweet and full of flavour, these muffins are sure to be a breakfast favourite. Bananas are the ultimate food fuel that will keep you feeling fuller for longer. Raisins add sweetness and, like bananas, are full of nutritional value.

MAKES 10

250g/9oz/2¼ cups plain (all-purpose) flour
5ml/1 tsp baking powder
5ml/1 tsp bicarbonate of soda (baking soda)
pinch of salt
2.5ml/½ tsp ground cinnamon

pinch of grated nutmeg
3 large ripe bananas
1 egg
70g/2½ oz/5 tbsp dark brown sugar
50ml/2fl oz/¼ cup vegetable oil
30g/1oz raisins

1 Preheat the oven to 190°C/375°F/Gas 5. Lightly grease the cups of a muffin tin (pan) or line them with paper cases.

2 Into a bowl, sift together the flour, baking powder, bicarbonate of soda, salt, cinnamon and nutmeg. Set aside.

3 Peel the bananas and chop them into another bowl. With an electric mixer, beat the bananas at moderate speed until mashed.

4 Beat the egg, sugar and oil into the mashed bananas.

5 Add the dry ingredients and beat in gradually, on low speed. Mix until just blended. Stir in the raisins.

6 Fill the prepared cups two-thirds full. For even baking, half-fill any empty cups with water. Bake until the tops spring back when touched lightly, around 20–25 minutes.

7 Leave in the tin to set for a few minutes. Transfer to a rack to cool. Eat when at room temperature or cold. Store in an airtight container for up to 3 days.

Nutritional information per portion: Energy 187kcal/788kJ; Protein 3.4g; Carbohydrate 35.8g, of which sugars 16g; Fat 4.3g, of which saturates 0.6g; Cholesterol 19mg; Calcium 45mg; Fibre 1.2g; Sodium 10mg.

Spiced banana nut muffins

Packed with soft and dense mashed banana, the addition of chopped hazelnuts provides these delightful muffins with an added crunch and the mixed spice brings depth of flavour.

MAKES 12

75g/3oz/¾ cup wholemeal
    (whole-wheat) flour
50g/2oz/½ cup plain (all-purpose) flour
10ml/2 tsp baking powder
5ml/1 tsp mixed (apple pie) spice
50g/2oz/¼ cup soft light brown sugar
50g/2oz/¼ cup butter, melted
1 egg, beaten
150ml/¼ pint/⅔ cup milk
grated rind of 1 orange
1 ripe banana
20g/¾oz/¼ cup rolled oats
20g/¾oz/scant ¼ cup chopped hazelnuts

1 Preheat the oven to 200°C/400°F/Gas 6. Line the cups of a muffin tin (pan) with paper cases.

2 Sift together both flours, the baking powder and mixed spice into a bowl, then add the bran remaining in the sieve (strainer). Stir in the sugar.

3 Pour the melted butter into a mixing bowl. Allow to cool slightly, then beat in the egg, milk and grated orange rind.

4 Gently fold in the dry ingredients. Mash the banana, then stir it into the batter. Do not overmix it. Spoon into the prepared paper cases.

5 Combine the oats and hazelnuts and sprinkle a little over each muffin. Bake for 20 minutes until the muffins are well risen and golden. Leave to stand for a few minutes, then transfer to a wire rack and serve warm or cold. Store in an airtight container for up to 3 days.

Nutritional information per portion: Energy 152kcal/642kJ; Protein 2.8g; Carbohydrate 29g, of which sugars 13.9g; Fat 3.6g, of which saturates 0.5g; Cholesterol 16mg; Calcium 34mg; Fibre 1g; Sodium 9mg.

Spiced sultana muffins

Weekend breakfasts will never be the same again once you have tried these delicious muffins!
They are quick and easy to prepare and take only a short time to bake.

MAKES 6

75g/3oz/6 tbsp butter, melted
1 small (US medium) egg
120ml/4fl oz/¹⁄₂ cup unsweetened
    coconut milk
150g/5oz/1¹⁄₄ cups wholemeal
    (whole-wheat) flour
5ml/1 tsp baking powder
7.5ml/1¹⁄₂ tsp ground cinnamon
115g/4oz/²⁄₃ cup sultanas
    (golden raisins)

1 Preheat the oven to 190°C/
375°F/Gas 5. Lightly grease the
cups of a muffin tin (pan) or line
them with paper cases.

2 Put the butter, egg and coconut
milk in a large bowl and beat
together until well blended.

3 Next sift the flour, baking powder
and cinnamon over the beaten
mixture. Fold in gently.

4 Add the sultanas and fold in.
Divide the batter among the
muffin cups.

5 Bake for 20 minutes or until the
muffins have risen well and are firm
to the touch.

6 Cool slightly on a wire rack
before serving. Store the muffins
in an airtight container for up
to 3 days.

Nutritional information per portion: Energy 240kcal/1006kJ; Protein 4.9g; Carbohydrate 30.3g, of which sugars 14.9g;
Fat 11.9g, of which saturates 6.9g; Cholesterol 58mg; Calcium 35mg; Fibre 2.6g; Sodium 114mg.

Rhubarb muffins with ginger

The shiny candied strips of scarlet rhubarb and paper-thin slices of stem ginger add a sweet, colourful topping to these muffins. Use extra stem ginger to decorate the cooled muffins, if you like.

MAKES 9–10 TALL MUFFINS

275g/10oz rhubarb, cleaned
30ml/2 tbsp syrup from a jar
   of preserved stem ginger
1 piece preserved stem ginger, chopped
50g/2oz/4 tbsp demerara (raw) sugar
150g/5oz/1¼ cups plain
   (all-purpose) flour
75g/3oz/¾ cup wholemeal
   (whole-wheat) or spelt flour
50g/2oz/¼ cup caster (superfine) sugar
10ml/2 tsp baking powder

2.5ml/½ tsp bicarbonate of soda
   (baking soda)
5ml/1 tsp ground ginger
120ml/4fl oz/½ cup natural (plain) yogurt
1 egg, lightly beaten

FOR THE TOPPING

15g/½oz/1 tbsp butter
15ml/1 tbsp ginger syrup
15ml/1 tbsp caster (superfine) sugar
1 piece stem ginger, finely sliced

1 Slice 175g/6oz rhubarb and put in a pan with 30ml/2 tbsp water, the ginger syrup, stem ginger and demerara sugar. Bring to the boil, stirring. Lower the heat and simmer until soft, 2–3 minutes. Set aside. Preheat the oven to 180°C/350°F/Gas 4.

2 Line dariole moulds or tall muffin tins (pans) with tall paper cases. Sift the dry ingredients into a bowl. In another bowl, beat the yogurt and egg together.

3 Stir the cooked rhubarb and juices into the yogurt and egg mixture and mix into the dry ingredients. Divide the batter between the paper cases.

4 To make the topping, heat the butter, ginger syrup, 15ml/1 tbsp water and sugar in a small frying pan over a medium heat and stir until the sugar dissolves. Cut the rest of the rhubarb into short fine strips and lightly stir them into the syrup.

5 Leave to soften for 2 minutes, then add the stem ginger slices until warmed through. Remove from the heat. Add in small piles to the centre of the muffin tops and bake for 20 minutes until golden.

Nutritional information per portion: Energy 152kcal/646kJ; Protein 3.9g; Carbohydrate 31.1g, of which sugars 15g; Fat 2.3g, of which saturates 1.1g; Cholesterol 23mg; Calcium 82mg; Fibre 1.5g; Sodium 42mg.

Blueberry breakfast cups

The perfect breakfast treat is a blueberry muffin baked in an ovenproof coffee cup.
Serve warm with a drizzle of maple syrup, if you like, and your favourite fresh ground coffee.

MAKES 16

450g/1lb/4 cups plain (all-purpose) flour
175g/6oz/³/4 cup butter, diced
30ml/2 tbsp baking powder
pinch of salt
275g/10oz/1¹/3 cups caster
   (superfine) sugar
275g/10oz/1¹/3 cups fresh blueberries
4 eggs
400ml/14fl oz/1²/3 cups buttermilk
maple syrup, to serve (optional)

1 Preheat the oven to 180°C/350°F/Gas 4. Use 175ml/6fl oz/³/4 cups capacity ovenproof cups and line with large paper cases.

2 Sift the flour into a bowl. Add the butter and rub it into the flour to form very fine breadcrumbs. Sift the baking powder, salt and sugar into the flour and butter mixture, then add the fresh blueberries.

3 Stir well to combine the ingredients evenly. Stir in the eggs and buttermilk, until just combined.

4 Spoon the batter into the paper cases until almost full and bake for 25 minutes, until a skewer inserted into the centre comes out clean.

5 Leave to stand and set in the cups for a few minutes before serving.

Nutritional information per portion: Energy 236kcal/992kJ; Protein 4.9g; Carbohydrate 34.7g, of which sugars 12.4g; Fat 9.6g, of which saturates 5.6g; Cholesterol 54mg; Calcium 88mg; Fibre 1.4g; Sodium 82mg.

Apricot and orange buns

These moreish muffins are ideal as a late breakfast. They are finished with a slightly sour orange glaze that perfectly complements the sweetness of the cakes.

MAKES 9–10

1 egg, lightly beaten
175ml/6fl oz/¾ cup buttermilk
juice and rind of 1½ Seville
    (Temple) oranges
75g/3oz/6 tbsp butter, melted
225g/8oz/2 cups plain (all-purpose) flour
10ml/2 tsp baking powder
150g/5oz/¾ cup golden caster
    (superfine) sugar
15ml/1 tbsp Seville orange marmalade
115g/4oz dried apricots, chopped

FOR THE ORANGE GLAZE
juice and finely grated rind of ½ Seville
    (Temple) orange
75–90ml/5–6 tbsp icing (confectioners')
    sugar, sifted
5ml/1 tsp Seville orange marmalade

1 Preheat the oven to 180°C/350°F/Gas 4. Line the cups of a muffin tin (pan) with paper cases. In a bowl, mix together the egg, buttermilk, orange juice and grated rind and the cooled, melted butter.

2 Sift the flour with the baking powder into a large mixing bowl and stir in the sugar. Make a well in the centre of the dry ingredients. Pour in the buttermilk mixture and fold it in gently, with the marmalade and the chopped apricots, until just blended. Do not overmix.

3 Spoon the batter into the prepared paper cases, filling them almost to the top. Bake for 25 minutes until the cakes look golden and puffed up. Leave to stand in the tin for 5 minutes, then turn out on to a wire rack to go cold.

4 To make the glaze, put the juice in a bowl and beat in the grated rind, icing sugar and marmalade. The mixture should cover the back of a spoon, but still be thin and fluid. Drizzle over the cakes 10 minutes before serving, so it is fresh and shiny. Serve immediately, or store without the glaze for up to 3 days.

Nutritional information per portion: Energy 211kcal/889kJ; Protein 3.5g; Carbohydrate 35.7g, of which sugars 18.6g; Fat 7g, of which saturates 4.3g; Cholesterol 37mg; Calcium 66mg; Fibre 0.7g; Sodium 75mg.

Apple and cranberry muffins

Sweet and sharp and decidedly moreish, these muffins are richly spiced and packed with plenty of fruit flavour. Cranberries are considered a superfood with many health-boosting properties.

MAKES 12

1 egg
50g/2oz/¼ cup butter, melted
100g/4oz/generous ½ cup caster
    (superfine) sugar
grated rind of 1 large orange
120ml/4fl oz/½ cup orange juice
140g/5oz/1¼ cups plain
    (all-purpose) flour
5ml/1 tsp baking powder
2.5ml/½ tsp ground cinnamon
2.5ml/½ tsp freshly grated nutmeg
2.5ml/½ tsp ground allspice
pinch of ground ginger
2 small eating apples
170g/6oz/1½ cups cranberries
55g/2oz/1⅓ cups walnuts, chopped

1 Preheat the oven to 180°C/350°F/ Gas 4. Grease the cups of a muffin tin (pan) or line with paper cases.

2 In a bowl, whisk the egg with the melted butter to combine. Add the sugar, grated orange rind and juice. Whisk to blend. Set aside.

3 In a large bowl, sift together the flour, baking powder, cinnamon, nutmeg, allspice, ginger and salt. Make a well in the dry ingredients and pour in the egg mixture. With a spoon, stir until just blended.

4 Peel, core and quarter the apples. Chop the apple flesh coarsely with a sharp knife.

5 Add the apples, cranberries and walnuts to the batter and stir lightly to blend.

6 Three-quarters fill the cups. Bake for 25–30 minutes, until golden. Leave the muffins to stand for 5 minutes before transferring to a wire rack to go cold. Store in an airtight container for up to 3 days.

Nutritional information per portion: Energy 149kcal/624kJ; Protein 2.5g; Carbohydrate 20.4g, of which sugars 10.8g; Fat 6.9g, of which saturates 2.6g; Cholesterol 25mg; Calcium 30mg; Fibre 0.9g; Sodium 34mg.

Pear and sultana bran muffins

These tasty fruit muffins are best eaten freshly baked and served warm or cold, spread with butter, and a dollop of your favourite jam or honey.

MAKES 12

75g/3oz/²/₃ cup wholemeal (whole-wheat) flour
50g/2oz/¹/₂ cup plain (all-purpose) flour
50g/2oz/scant ¹/₂ cup bran
15ml/1 tbsp baking powder
50g/2oz/¹/₄ cup butter, melted
50g/2oz/¹/₄ cup soft light brown sugar
1 egg, beaten
200ml/7fl oz/scant 1 cup milk
50g/2oz/¹/₂ cup ready-to-eat dried pears, chopped
50g/2oz/¹/₃ cup sultanas (golden raisins)

1 Preheat the oven to 200°C/400°F/Gas 6. Lightly grease the cups of a muffin tin (pan) or line them with paper cases.

2 Sift the wholemeal and plain flours, bran and baking powder into a large bowl.

3 In a jug (pitcher), mix together the melted butter, sugar, egg and milk and pour the mixture over the dry ingredients.

4 Gently fold the ingredients together. The mixture will be lumpy. Do not overmix.

5 Fold in the pears and sultanas. Spoon the batter into the prepared paper cases. Bake for 15–20 minutes, until risen and golden.

6 Leave to stand for a few minutes, then turn out on to a wire rack to cool. Store in an airtight container for up to 3 days.

Nutritional information per portion: Energy 121kcal/510kJ; Protein 3g; Carbohydrate 18.7g, of which sugars 9.8g; Fat 4.3g, of which saturates 2.4g; Cholesterol 25mg; Calcium 51mg; Fibre 2.2g; Sodium 42mg.

Berry brioche muffins

A traditional sweet brioche recipe is studded with fresh blueberries and makes an unusual and luxurious muffin. For a special breakfast treat, enjoy them warm spread with blueberry or cherry jam.

MAKES 10 LARGE MUFFINS

15g/½oz fresh yeast

4 medium (US large) eggs

350g/12oz/3 cups plain (all-purpose) flour

50g/2oz/¼ cup caster (superfine) sugar

10g/¼oz salt

175g/6oz/¾ cup unsalted butter, softened

115g/4oz/1 cup blueberries

45ml/3 tbsp milk, for the eggwash

1 small (US medium) egg yolk, for the eggwash

1 Crumble the yeast into the bowl of a food processor fitted with a dough hook. Add 10ml/2 tsp warm water and mix the two together.

2 Add the eggs, flour, sugar and salt. Beat at low speed for 6–7 minutes. Turn up to a moderate speed and gradually add the butter. Continue beating for 15 minutes until the dough is smooth and shiny. Seal in a plastic bag and chill for 24 hours, or overnight.

3 Lightly grease the cups of a muffin tin (pan). On a lightly floured surface, form the dough into a flattened sausage 10cm/4in wide.

4 Press the blueberries into the surface. Cut the dough into 10 equal-sized pieces. Using floured hands, form each into a ball, then press into a muffin cup.

5 Mix the milk and egg yolk together in a small bowl. Brush thinly over each of the muffins. Slash the tops twice with a sharp knife.

6 Preheat the oven to 220°C/425°F/Gas 7. Leave the dough in a warm place to prove for about 15 minutes, then bake for 13–15 minutes until golden and risen. Turn the muffins out on to a floured tray and leave to cool. Serve fresh for best results.

Nutritional information per portion: Energy 302kcal/1266kJ; Protein 6g; Carbohydrate 33.5g, of which sugars 7.1g; Fat 17g, of which saturates 10.2g; Cholesterol 117mg; Calcium 145mg; Fibre 1.3g; Sodium 288mg.

Savoury, vegetable and herb muffins

Perfect for serving for lunch with soup, pâté or

cheese, this delicious collection of muffin

recipes is guaranteed to please. As well as the

more traditional flavours of chilli and cheese,

there are unusual recipes for Bacon, Brie and

Fresh Date Muffins, and muffins flavoured

with wild mushrooms or mace. Muffins made with

vegetables and herbs have a moist texture, which

in turn gives them a longer shelf-life. Try scented

Marigold Flower Corn Muffins, or rich and

flavoursome Sweet Marrow Muffins.

Savoury cheese muffins

Puffed up and golden with their yummy cheese filling and the merest hint of hot spice, these must top the list of everyone's favourite savoury muffins. These muffins are best served warm.

MAKES 9

175g/6oz/1½ cups plain (all-purpose) flour
10ml/2 tsp baking powder
30ml/2 tbsp caster (superfine) sugar
5ml/1 tsp paprika
2 eggs
120ml/4fl oz/½ cup milk
50g/2oz/¼ cup butter, melted
5ml/1 tsp dried thyme
50g/2oz mature (sharp) Cheddar cheese, diced

1 Preheat the oven to 190°C/375°F/ Gas 5. Grease the cups of a muffin tin (pan) or line with paper cases.

2 Sift together the flour, baking powder, sugar and paprika. Make a well in the centre. Set aside.

3 Combine the eggs, milk, melted butter and dried thyme in another bowl and beat lightly with a whisk until thoroughly blended. Add the milk mixture to the dry ingredients.

4 Stir lightly with a wooden spoon until just combined. Do not overmix.

5 Place a heaped tablespoonful of the mixture in each of the prepared paper cases. Divide the pieces of cheese equally among the paper cases.

6 Top with another spoonful of the batter, covering the cheese. Bake for 25 minutes, until puffed and golden. Leave to stand for 5 minutes before moving to a wire rack to cool slightly.

Nutritional information per portion: Energy 166kcal/ 698kJ; Protein 5.1g; Carbohydrate 19.3g, of which sugars 4.4g; Fat 8.1g, of which saturates 4.6g; Cholesterol 60mg; Calcium 93mg; Fibre 0.6g; Sodium 96mg.

Chilli cheese muffins

Prepare for a whole new taste sensation with these fabulous spicy muffins – they're hot stuff. Sharp cheese, aromatic garlic and chilli purée combine in a muffin that is light but filling.

MAKES 12

115g/4oz/1 cup self-raising
　(self-rising) flour
15ml/1 tbsp baking powder
225g/8oz/2 cups fine cornmeal (polenta)
150g/5oz/1¼ cups grated mature
　(sharp) Cheddar cheese
50g/2oz/¼ cup butter, melted
2 eggs, beaten
5ml/1 tsp chilli purée (paste)
1 garlic clove, crushed
300ml/½ pint/1¼ cups milk

1 Preheat the oven to 200°C/400°F/ Gas 6. Line the cups of a muffin tin (pan) with paper cases.

2 Sift the flour and baking powder together into a bowl, then stir in the cornmeal and 115g/4oz/1 cup of the grated cheese until well mixed.

3 Stir together the melted butter, eggs, chilli purée, crushed garlic and milk until thoroughly combined.

4 Pour the liquid on to the dry ingredients and mix quickly until just combined.

5 Spoon the batter into the prepared paper cases and sprinkle the remaining grated cheese on top.

6 Bake for about 20 minutes, until risen and golden. Leave to cool for a few minutes before transferring to a wire rack to go cold, or serve warm.

Nutritional information per portion: Energy 166kcal/698kJ; Protein 5.1g; Carbohydrate 19.3g, of which sugars 4.4g; Fat 8.1g, of which saturates 4.6g; Cholesterol 60mg; Calcium 93mg; Fibre 0.6g; Sodium 96mg.

Shallot, thyme and garlic cheese muffins

These light muffins are best served warm, fresh from the oven, when the cream cheese and the caramelized flavour complement each other perfectly. Spread them with soft cheese for a mid-morning snack with a strong cup of coffee, or serve with soup, for lunch.

MAKES 10 TALL MUFFINS

225g/8oz shallots, peeled
25ml/1½ tbsp olive oil, for frying
15g/½oz/1 tbsp unsalted butter, for frying
10ml/2 tsp fresh thyme, plus a few sprigs
    for decoration
salt and ground black pepper
225g/8oz/2 cups self-raising (self-rising) flour

pinch of salt
10ml/2 tsp baking powder
10ml/2 tsp caster (superfine) sugar
115g/4oz soft herb and garlic cream cheese
175ml/6fl oz/¾ cup milk
2 eggs
75g/3oz/6 tbsp butter, melted

1 Preheat the oven to 180°C/350°F/Gas 4. Lightly grease and line 10 dariole moulds with baking parchment.

2 Drop the peeled shallots into a pan of boiling water and blanch them for 2 minutes. Drain thoroughly, then leave to stand on kitchen paper. When the shallots are cool enough to handle, slice them into quarters.

3 In a frying pan, heat the oil and butter over a medium heat. Add the shallots and sauté them until caramelized on all sides. Stir in the thyme and seasoning. Leave to cool.

4 In a large bowl, sift together the flour, salt, baking powder and sugar. In another bowl, beat together the cream cheese, milk, eggs and melted butter. Pour into a well in the centre of the dry ingredients and blend until partly mixed.

5 Scrape the shallots and any liquid into the batter (reserving a few of them for decorating) and stir lightly. Divide the batter between the moulds and dot with the reserved shallots and a few thyme sprigs.

6 Bake for 25–30 minutes or until the tops are firm to the touch. Leave to cool slightly, then invert on to a floured tray. Serve warm.

Nutritional information per portion: Energy 236kcal/984kJ; Protein 4.5g; Carbohydrate 20.7g, of which sugars 3.5g; Fat 15.6g, of which saturates 9g; Cholesterol 71mg; Calcium 124mg; Fibre 1g; Sodium 207mg.

Vegetable muffins

Onions, courgettes, cream cheese and herbs have a healthy appeal. When combined in these vegetarian muffins, they have a sharp and tangy flavour and a moist texture.

MAKES 8 TALL MUFFINS

250g/9oz/2¼ cups self-raising
   (self-rising) flour
pinch of celery salt or salt
12.5ml/2½ tsp baking powder
5ml/1 tsp caster (superfine) sugar
3.5ml/¾ tsp cayenne pepper
8 spring onions (scallions)
150g/5oz courgettes (zucchini), grated
30ml/2 tbsp red onion, grated
10ml/2 tsp malt vinegar
ground black pepper
115g/4oz/1 cup soft herb cream cheese
60ml/4 tbsp sour cream
75g/3oz/6 tbsp butter, melted
2 eggs
15ml/1 tbsp mixed fresh parsley and
   thyme, finely chopped
15g/½oz Parmesan cheese
olive oil, to drizzle

1 Preheat the oven to 180°C/350°F/ Gas 4. Grease and line 8 dariole moulds with baking parchment.

2 In a large bowl, sift together the flour, salt, baking powder, sugar and cayenne pepper and set aside.

3 Slice the white parts of the spring onions and mix with the grated courgettes and grated red onion. Sprinkle with the vinegar. Season and set aside to marinate.

4 Whisk the soft cheese into the sour cream, then whisk in the melted butter, eggs and herbs. Pour into the dry ingredients with the Parmesan and grated vegetables and any juices from the bowl. Stir to mix.

5 Fill the prepared paper cases three-quarters full. Drizzle lightly with olive oil. Add a few twists of black pepper and bake for 25–30 minutes. Leave to cool slightly, then transfer to a wire rack to go cold.

Nutritional information per portion: Energy 291kcal/1215kJ; Protein 6.8g; Carbohydrate 25.8g, of which sugars 1.9g; Fat 18.6g, of which saturates 11.1g; Cholesterol 126mg; Calcium 109mg; Fibre 1.4g; Sodium 154mg.

Walnut, cheese and barleycorn muffins

This recipe uses a mixture of self-raising and barleycorn flour, which contains mixed grains that provide texture as well as flavour. Chopped walnuts add extra crunch.

MAKES 8

115g/4oz/1 cup self-raising
   (self-rising) flour
10ml/2 tsp baking powder
3.5ml/³⁄₄ tsp cayenne pepper
150g/5oz/1¼ cups barleycorn bread flour
150g/5oz/1¼ cups mature (sharp)
   Cheddar cheese, grated
2 eggs
50ml/2fl oz/¼ cup milk
100ml/3½fl oz/scant ½ cup buttermilk
3.5ml/³⁄₄ tsp English mustard
75g/3oz/6 tbsp butter, melted
30ml/2 tbsp finely chopped fresh parsley
25g/1oz/1½ tbsp walnuts, chopped

1 Preheat the oven to 190°C/375°F/Gas 5. Lightly grease the cups of a muffin tin (pan), or line them with paper cases.

2 Sift the flour, baking powder, salt and cayenne into a mixing bowl. Stir in the barleycorn flour with the grated cheese until well combined.

3 In a small bowl, whisk the eggs, milk, buttermilk and mustard together. Mix in the melted butter.

4 Pour the liquid into the dry ingredients with the parsley. Fold in until half blended, then fold in the chopped walnuts.

5 Divide the batter equally between the paper cases and bake for 25 minutes, until golden on top and springy to the touch.

6 Leave the muffins in the tin for 5 minutes to cool slightly, then turn out on to a wire rack.

Nutritional information per portion: Energy 291kcal/1216kJ; Protein 9g; Carbohydrate 26.4g, of which sugars 1.6g; Fat 16.9g, of which saturates 9.6g; Cholesterol 41mg; Calcium 233mg; Fibre 2.8g; Sodium 272mg.

Broccoli and blue cheese muffins

Stilton, with its distinctive blue veins running through a round of cream-colour cheese, is perfect for these muffins, but you could use any sharp-tasting blue cheese.

MAKES 8

150g/5oz broccoli
30ml/2 tbsp olive oil, for frying
40g/1½ oz/3 tbsp butter, for frying
250g/9oz/2¼ cups self-raising
   (self-rising) flour
12.5ml/2½ tsp baking powder
30ml/2 tbsp sour cream
75g/3oz/6 tbsp butter, melted
45ml/3 tbsp milk
2 eggs
20ml/4 tsp sweet chilli dipping sauce
150g/5oz Stilton, such as Colston
   Bassett, grated

1 Preheat the oven to 180°C/350°F/Gas 4. Line the cups of a muffin tin (pan) with paper cases. Cut the broccoli florets into tiny pieces. Discard the stems.

2 In a frying pan, heat the oil and butter over a medium heat, add the broccoli and fry gently for 90 seconds, stirring. Scrape from the pan into a bowl and leave to cool.

3 Sift the flour and baking powder into a large bowl and set aside.

4 In a jug (pitcher), beat together the sour cream, melted butter, milk and eggs. Pour into the dry ingredients and partly combine. Stir in the broccoli, chilli sauce and Stilton, until just combined.

5 Spoon the batter into the paper cases. Bake for 25 minutes until golden and puffed up. Leave to stand in the tin for a few minutes, then transfer to a wire rack to cool.

Nutritional information per portion: Energy 346kcal/1441kJ; Protein 9.8g; Carbohydrate 24.4g, of which sugars 1.1g; Fat 23.6g, of which saturates 13.3g; Cholesterol 103mg; Calcium 199mg; Fibre 1.5g; Sodium 418mg.

Simple bacon muffins

Soft herb cream cheese and buttermilk are the basis for the 'savoury' flavour in this recipe, while the smoked bacon adds extra saltiness. Eat these muffins fresh for the best flavour.

MAKES 7

225g/8oz/2 cups self-raising (self-rising) flour

10ml/2 tsp baking powder

10ml/2 tsp maple syrup or caster (superfine) sugar

1 egg

75g/3oz/6 tbsp butter, melted

115g/4oz/½ cup soft garlic and herb cream cheese

175ml/6fl oz/¾ cup buttermilk

30ml/2 tbsp olive oil, for frying

15g/½oz/1 tbsp butter, for frying

225g/8oz very lean smoked bacon, plus extra to serve

maple syrup, to serve

1 Preheat the oven to 180°C/350°F/Gas 4. Line the cups of a muffin tin (pan) with paper cases. Sift the flour, baking powder and sugar, but not the maple syrup, into a bowl. Make a well in the centre.

2 Beat the egg, butter, cream cheese and buttermilk together in a bowl with the maple syrup, if using.

3 Heat the oil and butter over a medium heat and fry the bacon until it is lightly caramelized, about 4 minutes. Remove from the heat. Cut the bacon into tiny pieces and set aside a small quantity for serving.

4 Pour the wet ingredients into the well in the dry ingredients. Add the bacon and any juices from the pan. Mix until combined. Spoon the batter into the paper cases and bake for 25–30 minutes, until the muffins are golden.

5 Cool slightly. Serve warm, topped with the extra bacon and maple syrup.

Nutritional information per portion: Energy 395kcal/1644kJ; Protein 10.5g; Carbohydrate 27g, of which sugars 3.2g; Fat 28g, of which saturates 14.6g; Cholesterol 90mg; Calcium 167mg; Fibre 1g; Sodium 780mg.

Brioche muffins with savoury pâté stuffing

Serve these savoury brioche-style muffins with cold cuts of meat, quiche and salad at a picnic, or for an appetizer with a selection of toasted breads to accompany pâté. These muffins take time to prepare but the results are well worthwhile. Eat fresh, either warm or cold, for the best taste.

MAKES 10 TALL MUFFINS

15g/¹/₂oz fresh yeast

4 medium (US large) eggs

350g/12oz/3 cups plain
     (all-purpose) flour

35g/1¹/₄oz/3 tbsp caster (superfine) sugar

10g/¹/₄oz salt

175g/6oz/³/₄ cup unsalted butter, softened

150g/5oz fairly coarse pâté

45ml/3 tbsp milk

1 small (US medium) egg yolk

1 Crumble the yeast into the bottom of the bowl of a food processor fitted with a dough hook, and mix with 10ml/2 tsp warm water until well blended. Add the eggs, flour, sugar and salt.

2 Beat together at a low speed for 6–7 minutes until a dough forms. Turn up to a moderate speed and gradually add the butter. Continue to knead for 12–15 minutes until smooth and shiny. Seal the dough in a plastic bag and leave in the refrigerator for 24 hours.

3 Line the cups of individual dariole moulds with paper cases. Divide the pâté into 10 pieces, and with lightly floured hands, form them into balls. Set aside.

4 Place the dough on a floured work surface. Form it into a sausage and cut it into 10 equal pieces.

5 Add a ball of pâté to the centre of each piece of dough, then press the dough around the pâté to form a smooth ball. With the seal below, put the dough into the paper cases.

6 Preheat the oven to 220°C/425°F/Gas 7. In a small bowl, mix the milk and egg yolk together to make an egg wash. Using a pastry brush, apply it thinly over the top of each dough ball. With a sharp knife slash the top of each muffin twice. Leave in a warm place to prove for 15 minutes.

7 Bake for 13–15 minutes, until well risen and golden. Turn out the muffins with a sharp shake on to a floured tray and leave them to cool.

Nutritional information per portion: Energy 347kcal/1449kJ; Protein 8.3g; Carbohydrate 31.2g, of which sugars 4.5g; Fat 21.9g, of which saturates 11.6g; Cholesterol 162mg; Calcium 75mg; Fibre 1.1g; Sodium 282mg.

Bacon, mushroom and maple syrup muffins

These delicious muffins make the perfect treat on Sunday morning. Serve one or two of the freshly baked muffins per person on warmed plates and top with extra hot crispy bacon and a drizzle of warm maple syrup for a special occasion brunch.

MAKES 8–9 LARGE MUFFINS

225g/8oz/2 cups plain (all-purpose) flour

12.5ml/2½ tsp baking powder

30ml/2 tbsp olive oil, for frying

25g/1oz/2 tbsp butter, for frying

150g/5oz streaky (fatty) smoked bacon rashers (strips)

115g/4oz/1½ cups small flat mushrooms, thinly sliced

2 eggs

200ml/7fl oz/scant 1 cup buttermilk

75g/3oz/6 tbsp butter, melted

10ml/2 tsp maple syrup

extra rashers (strips) of streaky (fatty) bacon and maple syrup, to serve

1 Preheat the oven to 180°C/350°F/Gas 4. Lightly grease the cups of a muffin tin (pan).

2 In a large bowl, sift together the flour and baking powder.

3 In a pan, heat the oil and butter and fry the bacon gently until crisp, about 4 minutes. Remove from the heat. Cut into small strips, cover with foil and keep warm.

4 Return the pan to the heat and stir the mushrooms in the hot oil and butter for 30 seconds. Set them aside in the pan.

5 In a small bowl, beat the eggs, buttermilk and melted butter together. Pour the liquid into the dry ingredients with the maple syrup. Stir until partly combined.

6 Add the bacon and mushrooms and any juices from the pan and stir in. Do not overmix.

7 Fill the prepared muffin tin (pan) and bake for 25 minutes until well risen and firm to the touch. Leave to cool slightly then turn out on to a wire rack to cool. Serve immediately.

Nutritional information per portion: Energy 286kcal/1197kJ; Protein 7.5g; Carbohydrate 29.4g, of which sugars 10.3g; Fat 16.3g, of which saturates 8g; Cholesterol 78mg; Calcium 74mg; Fibre 0.9g; Sodium 399mg.

Corn muffins with ham

These delicious little muffins are perfect to serve as an appetizer with hot soup.
If you like, serve them unfilled with a pot of herb butter.

MAKES 24 MINI MUFFINS

50g/2oz/scant ¹/₂ cup yellow
    cornmeal (polenta)
65g/2¹/₂oz/generous ¹/₂ cup plain
    (all-purpose) flour, sifted
30ml/2 tbsp caster (superfine) sugar
7.5ml/1¹/₂ tsp baking powder
50g/2oz/¹/₄ cup butter, melted
120ml/4fl oz/¹/₂ cup whipping cream
1 egg
1–2 jalapeño or other medium-hot chillies,
    seeded and finely chopped (optional)
pinch of cayenne pepper
butter, for spreading
grainy mustard or mustard with honey,
    for spreading
50g/2oz oak-smoked ham, sliced, for filling

1 Preheat the oven to 200°C/400°F/ Gas 6. Lightly grease the cups of a mini muffin tin (pan) or line them with mini paper cases.

2 In a large bowl, combine the cornmeal, sifted flour, sugar and baking powder.

3 In another bowl, whisk together the melted butter, cream, egg, chopped chillies, if using, and the cayenne pepper.

4 Make a well in the cornmeal mixture, pour in the egg mixture and stir in just enough to blend (the batter does not have to be smooth).

5 Drop a spoonful of batter into each paper case. Bake for 12–15 minutes, until golden. Leave to stand for a few minutes in the tin, then transfer to a wire rack to go completely cold.

6 Split the muffins, spread with butter and mustard and sandwich with ham.

Nutritional information per portion: Energy 54kcal/227kJ; Protein 1.5g; Carbohydrate 6.8g, of which sugars 1.6g; Fat 2.5g, of which saturates 1.4g; Cholesterol 14mg; Calcium 13mg; Fibre 0.2g; Sodium 43mg.

Bacon, Brie and fresh date muffins

The strong flavours of bacon and fresh dates make a wonderful marriage. With the addition of Brie, these little muffins are unusual enough to serve in miniature form as tempting canapés.

MAKES 24–28 MINI MUFFINS

225g/8oz/2 cups plain (all-purpose) flour
pinch of salt
10ml/2 tsp baking powder
10ml/2 tsp caster (superfine) sugar
12 fresh dates, pitted and chopped
30ml/2 tbsp olive oil, for frying
15g/½ oz/1 tbsp butter, for frying
12 rashers (strips) smoked, streaky (fatty) bacon
75g/3oz Brie, diced
150ml/¼ pint/⅔ cup milk
50g/2oz/¼ cup butter, melted
2 eggs, beaten

1 Preheat the oven to 180°C/350°F/Gas 4. Lightly grease the cups of a mini muffin tin (pan) or line with paper cases.

2 Sift together the flour, salt, baking powder and sugar, add the chopped dates, and set aside.

3 Heat the oil and butter over a medium heat, and fry the bacon until crisp, 4 minutes. Cut the warm bacon into small pieces and stir it back into the warm juices in the pan. Cover with foil and set aside.

4 Mash the Brie as finely as you can into the milk, then mix it into the dry ingredients along with the melted butter, eggs, the fried bacon and any juices from the pan. Mix lightly together until just combined.

5 Fill the prepared paper cases three-quarters full. Bake for 18–20 minutes, until risen and golden.

6 Leave to stand and set for five minutes before turning out on to a wire rack. Serve warm, or store for up to 3 days in an airtight container.

Nutritional information per portion: Energy 183kcal/724kJ; Protein 4.9g; Carbohydrate 12.2g, of which sugars 0.6g; Fat 11.9.6g, of which saturates 8.3g; Cholesterol 53mg; Calcium 99mg; Fibre 0.8g; Sodium 202mg.

Devils on horseback

The very moreish combination of salty bacon and sweet fresh dates makes an unusual and seductive addition to these light and delicious muffins.

MAKES 10

225g/8oz/2 cups self-raising (self-rising) flour
10ml/2 tsp baking powder
10ml/2 tsp caster (superfine) sugar
12 rashers (strips) thin-cut smoked, streaky (fatty) bacon
24 fresh dates, pitted
30ml/2 tbsp olive oil, for frying

15g/½oz/1 tbsp butter, for frying
10ml/2 tsp fresh thyme or oregano, plus a few leaves for decoration
ground black pepper
115g/4oz/1 cup soft herb and garlic cream cheese
175ml/6fl oz/¾ cup milk
75g/3oz/6 tbsp butter, melted
2 eggs

1 Preheat the oven to 180°C/350°F/Gas 4. Line the cups of a muffin tin (pan) with baking parchment.

2 Sift the flour, baking powder and sugar into a mixing bowl. Using scissors, cut each bacon rasher in half and wrap one around each date.

3 In a frying pan, heat the oil and butter over a medium heat, and when it is foaming, add the bacon rolls and sauté them, turning them in the juices until they are crisp and caramelized on all sides, 4 minutes. Stir in the thyme or oregano and season with the pepper. Leave to cool slightly in the warm juices.

4 When cool enough to handle, slice each of the bacon-wrapped dates into 4 discs. Return them to the pan and cover with foil.

5 Beat the cream cheese into the milk, with the butter and eggs. Pour into the dry ingredients and stir lightly until part blended. Scrape the bacon and date slices with any of the cooking juices into the batter and stir until evenly combined. Avoid overmixing.

6 Divide the batter between the paper cases and dot with a few extra thyme leaves. Bake for 25 minutes or until the tops are golden. Leave the muffins to cool slightly, then turn out on to a wire rack to cool. Serve warm or cold.

Nutritional information per portion: Energy 318kcal/1327kJ; Protein 8g; Carbohydrate 23.6g, of which sugars 6.9g; Fat 22g, of which saturates 11g; Cholesterol 85mg; Calcium 124mg; Fibre 1g; Sodium 491mg.

Carrot muffins

Sweet and moist and subtly flavoured with cinnamon and nutmeg, these bitesize carrot muffins are perfect for a lunchbox treat. They're very addictive, so make plenty to share with friends.

MAKES 12

175g/6oz/³⁄₄ cup butter, softened
90g/3¹⁄₂oz/scant ¹⁄₂ cup soft dark
    brown sugar
1 egg
225g/8oz/1³⁄₄ cups carrots, grated
140g/5oz/1¹⁄₄ cups plain
    (all-purpose) flour
5ml/1 tsp baking powder
2.5ml/¹⁄₂ tsp bicarbonate of soda
    (baking soda)
5ml/1 tsp ground cinnamon
pinch of freshly grated nutmeg

1 Preheat the oven to 180°C/350°F/Gas 4. Lightly grease the cups of a muffin tin (pan).

2 Cream the butter and sugar until light and fluffy. Beat in the egg and 15ml/1 tbsp water. Stir in the carrots.

3 Sift over the flour, baking powder, bicarbonate of soda, cinnamon and nutmeg. Stir to blend.

4 Spoon the batter into the prepared tin, filling the cups almost full.

5 Bake until the tops spring back when touched lightly, about 35 minutes. Let the muffins stand for 10 minutes before transferring to a wire rack.

Nutritional information per portion: Energy 248kcal/1035kJ; Protein 3.6g; Carbohydrate 21.5g, of which sugars 15g; Fat 17g, of which saturates 4.4g; Cholesterol 36mg; Calcium 35mg; Fibre 1.6g; Sodium 47mg.

Pumpkin muffins

Small pumpkin varieties produce muffins with the sweetest taste. Select a pumpkin that is heavy for its size because it will have more moisture and be less likely to be stringy in texture.

MAKES 14

115g/4oz/½ cup butter, softened
150g/5oz/¾ cup soft dark brown sugar
60ml/4 tbsp molasses
225g/8oz cooked pumpkin
1 egg, beaten
225g/8oz/2 cups plain (all-purpose) flour
5ml/1 tsp bicarbonate of soda
    (baking soda)
7.5ml/1½ tsp ground cinnamon
5ml/1 tsp freshly grated nutmeg
25g/1oz/2 tbsp currants or raisins
butter, to serve

1 Preheat the oven to 200°C/400°F/Gas 6. Line the cups of a muffin tin (pan) with paper cases.

2 In a large bowl, beat the butter and sugar until light and fluffy. Beat in the molasses. Mash the pumpkin so that it is almost smooth (some lumps add to the texture), then add it with the egg to the butter and sugar mixture and stir until well blended.

3 Sift over the flour, bicarbonate of soda, cinnamon and nutmeg. Fold just enough to blend. Fold in the currants or raisins. Spoon the batter into paper cases, filling them three-quarters full.

4 Bake until the tops spring back when touched lightly, 12–15 minutes. Leave to stand for 5 minutes, then transfer to a wire rack to cool. Serve with butter.

Nutritional information per portion: Energy 216kcal/906kJ; Protein 2.2g; Carbohydrate 32.5g, of which sugars 21.5g; Fat 9.4g, of which saturates 5.7g; Cholesterol 36mg; Calcium 84mg; Fibre 0.7g; Sodium 86mg.

Wild mushroom and pine nut muffins

These light flavoured savoury muffins make attractive accompaniments to soft cheeses, pâtés and soups. The pine nuts are decorative as well as adding texture and crunch, and a delicious warm nutty flavour. Serve them freshly baked and warm to enjoy them at their best.

MAKES 6–7 LARGE MUFFINS

250g/9oz/2¼ cups self-raising (self-rising) flour
11.5ml/2¼ tsp baking powder
150g/5oz mixture of wild mushrooms
90g/3½oz/scant ½ cup butter, for frying
large pinch cayenne pepper
large pinch mace
50–75g/2–3oz/½–¾ cup pine nuts
30ml/2 tbsp olive oil
90ml/6 tbsp buttermilk
75g/3oz/6 tbsp butter, melted
2 eggs

1 Preheat the oven to 180°C/350°F/Gas 4. Lightly grease the cups of a muffin tin (pan).

2 In a large bowl, sift the flour and baking powder and set aside. Clean and slice the mushrooms.

3 In a frying pan, heat 75g/3oz/6 tbsp of the butter over a medium heat. When it is foaming, add the mushrooms. Season with cayenne pepper and mace. Fry gently, stirring, until just softened. Scrape into a bowl and set aside to cool.

4 Fry the pine nuts in the remaining butter and the olive oil for 30 seconds. Add to the mushrooms.

5 Beat together the buttermilk, melted butter and eggs in a bowl. Stir into the dry ingredients with the mushrooms and pine nuts.

6 Spoon the batter into the prepared muffin tins and bake in the oven for about 25 minutes until the tops are golden and firm. Leave to stand for 5 minutes to cool slightly, then serve warm.

Nutritional information per portion: Energy 399kcal/1660kJ; Protein 6.9g; Carbohydrate 28g, of which sugars 1.4g; Fat 29.6g, of which saturates 14.2g; Cholesterol 109mg; Calcium 154mg; Fibre 1.5g; Sodium 334mg.

Sweet potato and raisin muffins

Although it may seem surprising, sweet potatoes are a great vegetable to bake with. Their natural flavour and bright orange colouring is enhanced by the addition of raisins.

MAKES 12

225g/8oz sweet potato
350g/12oz/3 cups plain
   (all-purpose) flour
15ml/1 tbsp baking powder
1 egg, beaten
225g/8oz/1 cup butter, melted
250ml/8fl oz/1 cup milk
50g/2oz/scant ½ cup raisins
50g/2oz/¼ cup caster (superfine) sugar
icing (confectioners') sugar,
   for dusting

1 Cut the sweet potato into chunks and cook in boiling water for 45 minutes, or until very tender. Drain the potato and when cool enough to handle, peel off the skin. Place in a large bowl and mash well.

2 Preheat the oven to 220°C/425°F/Gas 7. Lightly grease the cups of a muffin tin (pan) or line them with paper cases.

3 Sift the flour and baking powder over the potato. Stir in, then beat in the egg. Whisk the butter and milk together then add to the batter.

4 Add the raisins and sugar and mix the ingredients together. Spoon the batter into the prepared paper cases, filling them almost to the top.

5 Bake for 25 minutes until golden. Leave to stand in the tin for 5 minutes before turning out on to a wire rack to cool. Dust with icing sugar and serve warm.

Nutritional information per portion: Energy 297kcal/1245kJ; Protein 4.4g; Carbohydrate 34.9g, of which sugars 9.8g; Fat 16.6g, of which saturates 10.5g; Cholesterol 60mg; Calcium 80mg; Fibre 1.4g; Sodium 169mg.

Sweet marrow muffins

Marrow, flaked almonds, golden syrup and vanilla make an unusual muffin with a delicate flavour. These muffins will remain moist for up to one week, if kept in an airtight container.

MAKES 10

300g/11oz marrow (large zucchini)
100ml/3½fl oz/½ cup olive oil
225g/8oz/generous 1 cup soft light
   brown sugar
2 small (US medium) eggs
7.5ml/1½ tsp vanilla extract
30ml/2 tbsp golden (light corn) syrup
175g/6oz/generous 1 cup sultanas
   (golden raisins)
50g/2oz/½ cup flaked (sliced) almonds
250g/9oz/½ cups self-raising
   (self-rising) flour
pinch of salt
7.5ml/1½ tsp mixed (pumpkin pie) spice

1 Preheat the oven to 180°C/350°F/Gas 4. Lightly grease the cups of a muffin tin (pan) or line them with paper cases.

2 To prepare the marrow, peel and remove the central core of seeds. Grate the flesh. Set aside on kitchen paper to drain.

3 In a bowl, beat the oil with the sugar, then add the eggs, one at a time, beating until the mixture forms a pale batter. Add the vanilla and golden syrup and stir well to combine. Add the grated marrow flesh and the sultanas, then stir in the flaked almonds.

4 Sift the flour, salt and spice together and fold the mixture lightly into the cake batter. Do not overmix. Divide the batter between the prepared paper cases.

5 Bake for 25–30 minutes, until risen and golden. Leave to stand for a few minutes before turning out on to a wire rack to cool completely.

Nutritional information per portion: Energy 338kcal/1427kJ; Protein 5.7g; Carbohydrate 57.8g, of which sugars 39.1g; Fat 11g, of which saturates 1.6g; Cholesterol 38mg; Calcium 137mg; Fibre 1.8g; Sodium 118mg.

Caramelized pear and herb muffins

Many muffins make excellent desserts and this is certainly one of them. Serve hot with crème fraîche or fresh vanilla custard. Spoonfuls of warm caramel sauce to drizzle on top add a touch of luxury. The sweetness is offset by the addition of aromatic rosemary and cumin. Eat fresh.

MAKES 6 LARGE MUFFINS

3 ripe pears, peeled

40g/1½ oz unsalted butter, for frying the pears

15ml/1 tbsp caster (superfine) sugar, for frying the pears

2 eggs

200ml/7fl oz/scant 1 cup buttermilk

5ml/1 tsp fresh rosemary, finely chopped, plus extra to decorate

75g/3oz/6 tbsp butter, melted

225g/8oz/2 cups plain (all-purpose) flour

10ml/2 tsp baking powder

150g/5oz/generous ½ cup caster (superfine) sugar

60ml/4 tbsp warm caramel sauce, to serve

5ml/1 tsp cumin seeds

1 Preheat the oven to 190°C/375°F/Gas 5. Lightly grease 6 large cups of a muffin tin (pan).

2 Cut the stalk end off the pears. Dice the flesh from the stalk end and set aside. Cut the rest of the pears in half and remove the cores. Slice the flesh.

3 Melt the butter in a frying pan. Add the pear slices, the sugar and 45ml/ 4 tbsp water. Fry gently for 6 minutes, or until the pears caramelize. Set aside.

4 Beat the eggs with the buttermilk and rosemary. Stir in the melted butter.

5 In a large bowl, sift together the flour, baking powder and sugar. Make a well in the centre. Pour the liquid into the dry ingredients and partly blend. Add the chopped pears and continue to mix lightly until the batter is evenly blended. Do not overmix.

6 Spoon the batter into the prepared muffin tins, half-filling them. Add two caramelized pear segments to each. Add a teaspoon of caramel sauce and smooth with a knife. Sprinkle over the cumin seeds.

7 Bake for 25–30 minutes, or until a skewer inserted in the centre of a muffin comes out clean, and the tops are springy to the touch. Leave to cool slightly in the tin, then transfer to warmed plates. Decorate with fresh rosemary, drizzle with a little extra warmed caramel sauce and serve immediately.

Nutritional information per portion: Energy 486kcal/2045kJ; Protein 7.3g; Carbohydrate 74.1g, of which sugars 45.5g; Fat 20g, of which saturates 12.2g; Cholesterol 113mg; Calcium 133mg; Fibre 2.8g; Sodium 192mg.

Courgette and raisin muffins

These muffins are delicious, so if you're a keen gardener with a glut of courgettes to use up, ring the changes by making a sweet treat. The muffins are baked in terracotta pots, which are available from good cookware shops. Keep for up to one week in an airtight container.

MAKES 10 LARGE MUFFINS

150g/5oz courgettes (zucchini)

115g/4oz/1 cup pine nuts

200g/7oz/1 cup caster (superfine) sugar

2 eggs

115g/4oz/½ cup butter, melted

175g/6oz/1½ cup plain (all-purpose) flour

7.5ml/1½ tsp baking powder

115g/4oz/scant 1 cup raisins

1 Preheat the oven to 180°C/350°F/Gas 4. Grease and line the terracotta pots with a square of baking parchment.

2 Cut each courgette into fine julienne strips, then place on to kitchen paper and set aside to drain.

3 Spread the pine nuts on to a baking sheet and bake for about 1½–2 minutes until golden (watch them carefully as they burn quickly).

4 In a large bowl, beat together the sugar and eggs for 1 minute. Add the melted butter and beat for another minute. Sift in the flour and baking powder. Fold in until partly blended.

5 Add the raisins, grated courgettes and the toasted pine nuts and stir until they are evenly blended. Do not overmix.

6 Spoon the batter into the prepared terracotta pots and bake for 25–30 minutes until well risen and golden and the tops spring back when touched.

7 Leave to stand for a few minutes, then turn out on to a wire rack to go cold or serve in the pots.

Nutritional information per portion: Energy 351kcal/1471kJ; Protein 5.2g; Carbohydrate 43.2g, of which sugars 29.8g; Fat 18.7g, of which saturates 7.1g; Cholesterol 65mg; Calcium 53mg; Fibre 1.1g; Sodium 109mg.

Cornmeal, orange and rosemary muffins

Cornmeal (sometimes called maize meal or polenta) provides these muffins with a glorious yellow crumb which is delicately flavoured with fresh rosemary.

MAKES 10–11 STANDARD MUFFINS

2 oranges
4 eggs
115g/4oz/²⁄₃ cup cornmeal (polenta)
115g/4oz/1 cup ground almonds
225g/8oz/generous 1 cup caster (superfine) sugar
15ml/1 tbsp fresh rosemary, finely chopped
75g/3oz/³⁄₄ cup self-raising (self-rising) flour

FOR THE SYRUP

50ml/2fl oz/¹⁄₄ cup orange juice
50g/2oz/¹⁄₄ cup caster (superfine) sugar
2.5ml/¹⁄₂ tsp fresh rosemary, finely chopped
rind of ¹⁄₄ orange, cut into very thin 2cm/³⁄₄ in long strips

1 Place the whole oranges in a pan of boiling water and leave to boil for 2 hours, until soft. Remove from the pan and leave to cool.

2 Preheat the oven to 180°C/350°F/ Gas 4. Line the cups of a muffin tin (pan) with paper cases.

3 Split the fruit. Remove the pips (seeds). Purée the orange and skin using a blender until smooth. Whisk together the purée, eggs, polenta, ground almonds and sugar.

4 Add the rosemary. Sift over the flour and stir in until just blended. Spoon the batter into the paper cases.

5 Bake for 25 minutes, until golden and springy. Leave in the tin to cool slightly, then turn on to a wire rack.

6 For the syrup, put 25ml/1¹⁄₂ tbsp water with the remaining ingredients in a pan. Bring slowly to the boil, stirring. Boil for 4 minutes. Remove from the heat. Prick the surface of the muffins and pour over syrup.

Nutritional information per portion: Energy 259kcal/ 1089kJ; Protein 6.4g; Carbohydrate 41.6g, of which sugars 28.6g; Fat 8.3g, of which saturates 1.1g; Cholesterol 69mg; Calcium 82mg; Fibre 1.5g; Sodium 54mg.

Marigold flower corn muffins

These are moist and light corn muffins, which are best served cold, spread with butter and a spoonful of jam. Make sure you use English marigolds (Calendula), not (Tagetes) French marigolds.

MAKES 5–6 TALL MUFFINS

50g/2oz/¼ cup butter, softened

90g/3½oz/½ cup caster
   (superfine) sugar

2 eggs

5ml/1 tsp finely grated lemon rind

40g/1½ oz sour cream

150g/5oz/1¼ cups plain
   (all-purpose) flour

10ml/2 tsp baking powder

25g/1oz ground almonds

50g/2oz/½ cup cornmeal (polenta)

45ml/3 tbsp orange juice

20–25 marigold flower petals

1 Preheat the oven to 180°C/350°F/Gas 4. Grease 5–6 dariole moulds and line with baking parchment.

2 In a large bowl, cream the butter and sugar until light and fluffy. Beat in the eggs, one at a time, adding 15ml/1 tbsp sifted flour with each egg to prevent the mixture curdling.

3 Stir in the lemon rind and sour cream. Sift the flour and baking powder into the mixture and fold in.

4 Stir in the ground almonds and cornmeal until just combined.

5 Add the orange juice, taking care not to overmix the ingredients. Spoon the batter into the prepared dariole moulds. Sprinkle over the marigold flower petals.

6 Bake for 22–25 minutes, until well risen and golden. Leave to cool slightly, then transfer to a wire rack to go cold.

Nutritional information per portion: Energy 303kcal/1271kJ; Protein 6.5g; Carbohydrate 42.4g, of which sugars 17.1g; Fat 12.9g, of which saturates 6.1g; Cholesterol 87mg; Calcium 71mg; Fibre 1.3g; Sodium 92mg.

Caraway seed muffins with lemon glaze

The tiny slender seed of the caraway plant has a distinctive aromatic scent and slightly hot flavour, which resembles aniseed when it is added to breads and cakes. Serve these muffins while they are warm. Spread with butter, or add the syrupy lemon glaze for a sweeter teatime treat.

MAKES 8 LARGE MUFFINS

175g/6oz/¾ cup butter, softened
175g/6oz/scant 1 cup caster (superfine) sugar
3 eggs, lightly beaten
225g/8oz/2 cups plain (all-purpose) flour
5ml/1 tsp baking powder
30ml/2 tbsp milk
5ml/1 tsp vanilla extract
15ml/1 tbsp caraway seeds

FOR THE LEMON GLAZE

75g/3oz/¾ cup icing (confectioners')
    sugar, sifted
10–15ml/2–3 tsp lemon juice

1 Preheat the oven to 180°C/350°F/Gas 4. Lightly grease the cups of a muffin tin (pan) or line them with paper cases.

2 In a mixing bowl, beat the butter and sugar until light and fluffy. Beat in the eggs, then sift over half of the flour and baking powder. Stir lightly to combine.

3 In a small bowl, whisk together the milk, vanilla and caraway seeds. Pour the liquid into the batter with the remaining flour. Mix lightly.

4 Divide the batter between the prepared cups and bake for 25 minutes, until springy to the touch. Leave to cool slightly, then transfer to a wire rack.

5 To make the topping, in a bowl, mix the glaze ingredients together with 15ml/1 tbsp boiling water until smooth and the consistency of thin cream. Drizzle over the tops of the warm cakes. Keep for up to 1 week.

Nutritional information per portion: Energy 168Kcal/697kJ; Protein 3g; Carbohydrate 11.9g, of which sugars 9.2g; Fat 12.4g, of which saturates 6g; Cholesterol 24mg; Calcium 94mg; Fibre 3.1g; Sodium 758mg.

Teatime treats

This delicious selection of cupcakes and muffins

offers plenty of variety to inspire you, such as

luscious chocolate and spice cakes, summery

fresh berry muffins and tangy citrus confections.

With a variety of ingredients including crunchy

nuts, chocolate chips and fresh fruit, there is

something for everyone. From simple Honey and

Spice Cakes to indulgent Espresso Cupcakes with

Maple Syrup, these recipes make a perfect

accompaniment to a cup of hot coffee or tea

at any time of the day.

Espresso cupcakes with maple syrup

Strong dark coffee and maple syrup give a bitter edge to the sweetness of these little cakes. Drizzle more maple syrup over them while they are still warm.

MAKES 12

250g/9oz/2¼ cups plain
   (all-purpose) flour
10ml/2 tsp baking powder
pinch of cinnamon
50g/2oz/¼ cup golden caster
   (superfine) sugar
75g/3oz/6 tbsp butter
1 egg
105ml/7 tbsp pure maple syrup,
   plus extra for drizzling
105ml/7 tbsp strong coffee
45ml/3 tbsp buttermilk

1 Preheat the oven to 180°C/350°F/Gas 4. Lightly grease the cups of a muffin tin (pan) or line them with paper cases.

2 Sift the flour, baking powder and cinnamon into a large mixing bowl and then mix in the sugar.

3 Melt the butter in a small pan over a low heat, pour it into another mixing bowl and leave to cool.

4 Beat the egg and stir it into the butter. Add the maple syrup, coffee and buttermilk and combine.

5 Fold the egg mixture lightly into the dry ingredients until just combined. Do not overmix.

6 Spoon the mixture into the cases and bake for about 25 minutes. Serve the cupcakes with extra maple syrup drizzled over the top.

Nutritional information per portion: Energy 167kcal/703kJ; Protein 2.7g; Carbohydrate 27.6g, of which sugars 11.8g; Fat 5.9g, of which saturates 3.6g; Cholesterol 30mg; Calcium 42mg; Fibre 0.7g; Sodium 79mg.

Coffee and macadamia muffins

These creamy and crunchy muffins are good eaten cold, but are best served still warm from the oven. For the ultimate indulgence, serve them freshly baked with a strong black espresso.

MAKES 12

25ml/1½ tbsp ground coffee
250ml/8fl oz/1 cup milk
50g/2oz/¼ cup butter
275g/10oz/2½ cups plain
   (all-purpose) flour
10ml/2 tsp baking powder
150g/5oz/generous ½ cup light
   muscovado (brown) sugar
75g/3oz/generous ½ cup
   macadamia nuts
1 egg, lightly beaten

1 Preheat the oven to 200°C/400°F/Gas 6. Lightly grease the cups of a muffin tin (pan) or line them with paper cases.

2 Put the ground coffee in a jug (pitcher). Heat the milk to near-boiling and pour it over. Leave to infuse for 4 minutes, then strain into a mixing bowl. Discard the coffee grounds.

3 Add the butter to the coffee milk and stir until melted. Set aside and leave to cool. Sift the flour and baking powder into a large mixing bowl. Stir the sugar and macadamia nuts into the flour mixture. Make a well in the centre.

4 Add the egg to the coffee-flavoured milk mixture, pour into the dry ingredients and stir until just combined – do not overmix.

5 Divide the batter between the prepared paper cases and bake for 15 minutes until well risen and firm. Transfer to a wire rack to cool completely. The muffins will keep for up to three days in an airtight container.

Nutritional information per portion: Energy 221kcal/929kJ; Protein 4g; Carbohydrate 32.2g, of which sugars 14.7g; Fat 9.4g, of which saturates 3.3g; Cholesterol 26mg; Calcium 70mg; Fibre 1g; Sodium 59mg.

Honey and spice cakes

These little golden cakes are fragrant with honey and cinnamon. They tend to rise higher (and are therefore lighter) when they are baked in paper cases.

MAKES 18

250g/9oz/2¼ cups plain
    (all-purpose) flour
5ml/1 tsp ground cinnamon
5ml/1 tsp bicarbonate of soda
    (baking soda)
125g/4½ oz/½ cup butter, softened
125g/4½ oz/10 tbsp soft dark
    brown sugar
1 egg, separated
125g/4½ oz/10 tbsp clear honey
60ml/4 tbsp milk

1 Preheat the oven to 200°C/400°F/ Gas 6. Butter the cups of two bun tins (pans) or line them with paper cake cases. Sift the flour into a large bowl, together with the ground cinnamon and the bicarbonate of soda.

2 Beat the butter with the sugar in another bowl until the mixture is very light and fluffy. Beat in the egg yolk, then gradually add the honey.

3 Fold the flour, spice and bicarbonate of soda into the mixture until just combined.

4 Add sufficient milk from the measured amount to make a soft mixture that will just drop off the spoon.

5 In a separate bowl, whisk the separated egg white until stiff peaks form. Fold the egg white gently into the cake mixture.

6 Divide the mixture among the tins or cases. Bake for 25 minutes, until lightly coloured. Leave to stand for 5 minutes before transferring to a wire rack to cool.

Nutritional information per portion: Energy 152kcal/639kJ; Protein 1.9g; Carbohydrate 23.6g, of which sugars 13g; Fat 6.3g, of which saturates 3.8g; Cholesterol 26mg; Calcium 30mg; Fibre 0.4g; Sodium 49mg.

Snowballs

These snowy muffins prove that variations on this simple theme appear to be endless. They are topped with white chocolate mixed with coconut liqueur and cream, then sprinkled with coconut strands.

MAKES 12

175g/6oz/6 tbsp caster (superfine) sugar
2.5ml/½ tsp baking powder
200g/7oz/1¾ cups self-raising (self-rising) flour
15ml/1 tbsp desiccated (dry unsweetened shredded) coconut
175g/6oz/¾ cup soft tub margarine
3 eggs, beaten
15ml/1 tbsp milk

FOR THE TOPPING

175g/6oz white chocolate, chopped
15ml/1 tbsp coconut liqueur
75ml/5 tbsp double (heavy) cream
175g/6oz/2 cups large shredded coconut strands or curls

1 Preheat the oven to 180°C/ 350°F/Gas 4. Line a 12-cup deep muffin tray with paper cases.

2 Sift the sugar, baking powder, flour and coconut into a large bowl. Add the margarine, eggs and milk and beat until smooth and creamy.

3 Divide the batter evenly among the paper cases. Bake for 20 minutes, or until risen, golden and firm to the touch. Leave in the tin for 2 minutes, then turn out to cool on a wire rack.

4 To make the topping, put the chocolate and liqueur in a bowl. Put the cream in a pan and bring to the boil, then pour over the chocolate and liqueur. Stir until smooth, then cool and chill for 30 minutes.

5 Whisk with an electric mixer for a few minutes, or until light and fluffy. Spread the icing over the top of each muffin.

6 Sprinkle coconut strands liberally over the icing to cover completely.

Nutritional information per portion: Energy 481kcal/2005kJ; Protein 5.9g; Carbohydrate 39.6g, of which sugars 35.2g; Fat 34.3g, of which saturates 23.9g; Cholesterol 12mg; Calcium 137mg; Fibre 3g; Sodium 167mg.

Walnut and pecan muffins

Mini flowerpots are not only for gardeners. Heat-resistant terracotta pots are available in cookware shops for baking bread and can also be used for muffins. Make sure to line them well.

MAKES 16

450g/1lb/4 cups plain (all-purpose) flour
175g/6oz/¾ cup butter, diced
30ml/2 tbsp baking powder
pinch of salt
275g/10oz/1⅓ cups caster
    (superfine) sugar
rind of 1 large orange, finely grated
50g/2oz/4 tbsp sesame seeds
365g/13oz/3¼ cups mixed walnuts and
    pecans, finely chopped
4 eggs
400ml/14fl oz/1⅔ cups buttermilk

1 Preheat the oven to 180°C/350°F/Gas 4. Cut baking parchment into 12.5cm/5in squares and press into the greased terracotta pots.

2 Sift the flour into a large mixing bowl. Add the butter and rub it into the flour to form very fine breadcrumbs. Sift the baking powder, salt and sugar into the flour and butter mixture, then add the orange rind, sesame seeds and mixed chopped nuts. Stir well to combine the ingredients evenly.

3 Mix the eggs and the buttermilk in a jug (pitcher) and add to the dry ingredients. Stir until just combined.

4 Spoon the batter into the paper cases until almost full and bake for 25 minutes, until a skewer inserted into the centre comes out clean. Leave to stand and set in the pots for a few minutes before serving warm.

Nutritional information per portion: Energy 225kcal/946kJ; Protein 4.6g; Carbohydrate 29g, of which sugars 14.7g; Fat 10.6g, of which saturates 3.1g; Cholesterol 41mg; Calcium 64mg; Fibre 0.9g; Sodium 45mg.

Nutty cakes with walnut liqueur

These spicy little cakes have a crunchy topping and moist crumb studded with chopped walnuts. Chop the nuts very coarsely to give the cakes plenty of texture.

MAKES 12

50g/2oz/4 tbsp butter, melted
2 eggs, beaten
175ml/6fl oz/¾ cup milk
30ml/2 tbsp walnut liqueur
225g/8oz/2 cups plain (all-purpose) flour
20ml/4 tsp baking powder
2.5ml/½ tsp mixed (apple pie) spice
115g/4oz/⅔ cup soft light brown sugar
75g/3oz/¾ cup chopped walnuts

1 Preheat the oven to 200°C/400°F/Gas 6. Line a muffin tin (pan) with paper cases. In a jug (pitcher) mix the butter, eggs, milk and liqueur.

2 Sift the flour, baking powder and mixed spice into a large bowl. Stir in the sugar and the chopped walnuts, reserving about 15ml/1 tbsp of each to sprinkle over the top of the cakes. Make a well in the centre.

3 Pour the butter mixture into the dry ingredients and stir for just long enough to combine the ingredients. Do not overmix: the nuts mean that the batter will be lumpy.

4 Fill the paper cases two-thirds full, then top with a sprinkling of the reserved sugar and walnuts. Bake for 15 minutes until the muffins have risen and are golden brown. Leave to stand for 5 minutes, then turn on to a wire rack to cool.

Nutritional information per portion: Energy 201kcal/844kJ; Protein 4.3g; Carbohydrate 26.3g, of which sugars 12g; Fat 9.1g, of which saturates 3g; Cholesterol 42mg; Calcium 60mg; Fibre 0.8g; Sodium 53mg.

Chocolate and walnut muffins

This muffin offers the perfect combination for chocoholics – cocoa powder and added chocolate chunks. The dense and sweet chocolate batter is not for the faint-hearted.

MAKES 12

175g/6oz/³⁄4 cup unsalted butter

140g/5oz/1¹⁄4 cups plain
   (semisweet) chocolate

200g/7oz/1 cup caster (superfine) sugar

55g/2oz/¹⁄4 cup soft dark brown sugar

4 eggs, beaten

5ml/1 tsp vanilla extract

2.5ml/¹⁄2 tsp almond extract

115g/4oz/1 cup self-raising
   (self-rising) flour

15ml/1 tbsp unsweetened cocoa powder

115g/4oz/²⁄3 cup walnuts, chopped

1 Preheat the oven to 180°C/350°F/Gas 4. Lightly grease the cups of a muffin tin (pan) or line them with paper cases.

2 Melt the butter with the chocolate in a heatproof bowl set over a pan of gently simmering water. Remove from the heat.

3 Stir the sugars into the chocolate mixture. Mix in the eggs, then add the vanilla and almond extracts. Sift over the flour and cocoa. Fold in gently along with the walnuts.

4 Fill the prepared cups with the mixture and bake until a skewer inserted in the centre comes out clean, 30–35 minutes.

5 Allow the muffins to stand and set in the tin for about 5 minutes before turning out on to a wire rack to cool completely.

Nutritional information per portion: Energy 374kcal/1563kJ; Protein 4.9g; Carbohydrate 37.1g, of which sugars 32.2g; Fat 24g, of which saturates 10.8g; Cholesterol 95mg; Calcium 46mg; Fibre 0.8g; Sodium 115mg.

Espresso coffee and mascarpone cupcakes

These indulgent cupcakes have a soft Italian cream cheese topping, with a pronounced coffee flavour. They make the perfect accompaniment to an afternoon coffee break.

MAKES 8–10

150g/5oz/10 tbsp butter, softened

200g/7oz/scant 1 cup golden caster
  (superfine) sugar

3 eggs

175g/6oz/³⁄₄ cup mascarpone

5ml/1 tsp grated lemon rind

30ml/2 tbsp buttermilk

15ml/1 tbsp unsweetened cocoa powder

25ml/1¹⁄₂ tbsp espresso coffee

15ml/1 tbsp Marsala

250g/9oz/2¹⁄₄ cups self-raising
  (self-rising) flour

FOR THE TOPPING

175g/6oz/³⁄₄ cup butter, softened

2.5ml/¹⁄₂ tsp finely grated lemon rind

350g/12oz/3 cups icing (confectioners')
  sugar, sifted

225g/8oz/1 cup mascarpone

10ml/2 tsp strong espresso coffee

1 Preheat the oven to 180°C/350°F/Gas 4. Line a muffin tin (pan) with paper cases.

2 Beat the butter and sugar together until light and creamy. Gradually beat in the eggs, one at a time, beating well after each addition. Stir in the mascarpone, lemon rind, buttermilk, cocoa, coffee and Marsala, then fold in the flour.

3 Fill the prepared paper cases. Bake for 25 minutes, or until firm to the touch. Turn out on to a wire rack to cool.

4 Meanwhile make the topping. Beat the butter in a bowl until soft. Add the lemon rind and gradually mix in the sugar and mascarpone alternately, in small amounts, until smooth and creamy. Stir in the coffee.

5 Spoon the topping on to the top of each of the cakes, and dust with a little cocoa powder.

Nutritional information per portion: Energy 167kcal/703kJ; Protein 2.7g; Carbohydrate 27.6g, of which sugars 11.8g; Fat 5.9g, of which saturates 3.6g; Cholesterol 30mg; Calcium 41mg; Fibre 0.7g; Sodium 79mg.

Raspberry and white chocolate muffins

White chocolate and fresh raspberries make a combination that works particularly well in muffins. For a special occasion add a white chocolate truffle to the batter before baking.

MAKES 8 LARGE MUFFINS

225g/8oz/2 cups plain (all-purpose) flour

15ml/1 tbsp baking powder

115g/4oz/generous ½ cup caster (superfine) sugar

20g/¾oz/scant ¼ cup ground almonds

50g/2oz white, or white vanilla chocolate, finely chopped

2 eggs, beaten

75g/3oz/scant ½ cup butter, melted

50ml/2fl oz/¼ cup vegetable oil

30ml/2 tbsp milk

150g/5oz/scant 1 cup raspberries

FOR THE CHOCOLATE TRUFFLES

150ml/¼ pint/⅔ cup double (heavy) cream

5ml/1 tsp finely grated orange rind

350g/12oz white chocolate

50g/2oz/¼ cup butter

icing (confectioners') sugar

1 For the truffles, bring the cream to the boil and stir in the orange rind. Cool for 2 minutes. Add the white chocolate. Stir until it melts. Add the butter and continue to stir until smooth and glossy. Cool over a bowl of iced water, stirring until it begins to thicken (15–30 minutes).

2 Scoop 8 balls of the mixture on to a baking sheet lined with silicone paper. Chill for 2 hours until set.

3 Preheat the oven to 180°C/350°F/Gas 4. Line the cups of a muffin tin (pan) with paper cases. Sift the flour, baking powder and sugar into a large bowl. Stir in the ground almonds and the chocolate.

4 Mix together the eggs, butter and oil. Pour into the dry ingredients. Fold in with the milk until partly combined. Fold in the raspberries. Divide half the batter between the paper cases. Press a truffle into each. Fill with the remaining batter.

5 Bake for 25 minutes, until risen and springy to the touch. Leave to stand for a few minutes, then turn on to a wire rack to cool completely.

Nutritional information per portion: Energy 694kcal/2896kJ; Protein 9.6g; Carbohydrate 67.8g, of which sugars 46.3g; Fat 45.7g, of which saturates 24.2g; Cholesterol 108mg; Calcium 216mg; Fibre 1.5g; Sodium 201mg.

Gooey butterscotch cakes

If you like, you can make up the two mixtures for these cakes the night before you need them and stir them together first thing next day for an irresistible mid-morning treat.

MAKES 9–12

150g/5oz butterscotch sweets (candies)

225g/8oz/2 cups plain (all-purpose) flour

90g/3½ oz/½ cup golden caster (superfine) sugar

10ml/2 tsp baking powder

pinch of salt

1 egg, beaten

150ml/¼ pint/⅔ cup milk

50ml/2fl oz/¼ cup sunflower oil or melted butter

75g/3oz/¾ cup chopped hazelnuts

1 Preheat the oven to 200°C/400°F/Gas 6. Arrange 9–12 paper cases in a muffin tin (pan).

2 With floured fingers, break the butterscotch sweets into small chunks. Toss them in a little flour, if necessary, to prevent them from sticking together.

3 Sift the flour into a large mixing bowl, then sift in the sugar, baking powder and salt.

4 Whisk together the egg, milk and oil or melted butter, then lightly stir the mixture into the dry ingredients with the sweets and nuts.

5 Spoon the batter into the paper cases, filling about half full.

6 Bake for 20 minutes, until risen and golden. Leave the muffins to cool slightly in the tin for about 5 minutes, then remove and transfer them to a wire rack to cool completely.

Nutritional information per portion: Energy 224kcal/941kJ; Protein 3.9g; Carbohydrate 31.7g, of which sugars 14.6g; Fat 10g, of which saturates 2.1g; Cholesterol 19mg; Calcium 66mg; Fibre 1g; Sodium 55mg.

Little Madeira cakes with cream and jam

This recipe looks as good as it tastes. The Madeira cake mixture, enriched with ground almonds and Calvados, rises beautifully into a perfect dome. When the cakes have cooled the domes are carefully sliced away to make room for a mouthwatering filling of buttercream and raspberry jam.

MAKES 14

225g/8oz/1 cup butter, softened
225g/8oz/1 cup caster (superfine) sugar
4 eggs
225g/8oz/2 cups self-raising (self-rising) flour
115g/4oz/1 cup plain (all-purpose) flour
60ml/4 tbsp ground almonds
5ml/1 tsp finely grated lemon rind
30ml/2 tbsp Calvados, brandy or milk

FOR THE FILLING

175g/6oz/¾ cup butter, softened
350g/12oz/3 cups icing (confectioners') sugar,
    double sifted, plus extra for dusting
20ml/4 tsp lemon juice
20ml/4 tsp warm water
60ml/4 tbsp raspberry jam

1 Preheat the oven to 180°C/350°F/Gas 4. Line 14 cups of two muffin tins (pans) with paper cases.

2 Cream the butter and caster sugar together until light and fluffy. Add two of the eggs, a little at a time, mixing well after each addition. Sprinkle 15ml/1 tbsp of the flour into the mixture and beat it in.

3 Add the remaining eggs gradually, beating well after each addition, then beat in another 15ml/1 tbsp flour until just combined. Sift the remaining flours into the mixture and fold in lightly with the ground almonds, lemon rind and Calvados, brandy or milk.

4 Fill the prepared cups almost to the top. Bake for 20–22 minutes until the tops spring back when touched and the cakes are light golden. Transfer to a wire rack.

5 To make the buttercream, beat the softened butter with the icing sugar until it is smooth and fluffy. Stir in the lemon juice and warm water and continue to beat until smooth.

6 When the cakes have cooled completely, slice a round from the top of each. Using a large piping (pastry) bag fitted with a plain nozzle, pipe a circle of buttercream. Add a spoonful of jam to fill each cake before replacing the dome on top. Just before serving, dust lightly with sifted icing sugar.

Nutritional information per portion: Energy 574kcal/2406kJ; Protein 5.2g; Carbohydrate 75.5g, of which sugars 54g; Fat 29.5g, of which saturates 18.6g; Cholesterol 140mg; Calcium 81mg; Fibre 0.9g; Sodium 278mg.

Chocolate chip cakes

Nothing could be easier – or nicer – than these classic cakes. The muffin mixture is plain, but has a surprise layer of chocolate chips inside. Sprinkle a few chocolate chips on top of the cakes.

MAKES 10

115g/4oz/½ cup butter, softened
75g/3oz/⅓ cup caster (superfine) sugar
30ml/2 tbsp soft dark brown sugar
2 eggs
175g/6oz/1½ cups plain
    (all-purpose) flour
5ml/1 tsp baking powder
120ml/4fl oz/½ cup milk
175g/6oz/1 cup plain (semisweet)
    chocolate chips

1 Preheat the oven to 190°C/375°F/Gas 5. Arrange 10 paper cases in a muffin tin (pan).

2 In a large bowl, beat the butter until it is pale and light. Add the caster and dark brown sugars and beat until the mixture is light and fluffy. Beat in the eggs, one at a time, beating thoroughly after each addition.

3 Sift the flour and baking powder together twice. Fold into the butter mixture, alternating with the milk.

4 Divide half the mixture among the paper cases. Sprinkle with half the chocolate chips, then cover with the remaining mixture and the rest of the chocolate chips. Bake for about 25 minutes, until golden. Leave to stand for 5 minutes, then transfer to a wire rack to cool.

Nutritional information per portion: Energy 296kcal/1241kJ; Protein 4.2g; Carbohydrate 36.5g, of which sugars 22.3g; Fat 15.9g, of which saturates 9.5g; Cholesterol 67mg; Calcium 59mg; Fibre 0.5g; Sodium 110mg.

Chunky chocolate and banana cupcakes

Luxurious but not overly sweet, these cakes are simple and quick to make. They taste best if served while still warm, when the chocolate is soft and gooey.

MAKES 12

90ml/6 tbsp semi-skimmed
   (low-fat) milk
2 eggs
150g/5oz/²⁄₃ cup butter, melted
225g/8oz/2 cups plain (all-purpose) flour
5ml/1 tsp baking powder
150g/5oz/³⁄₄ cup golden caster
   (superfine) sugar
150g/5oz plain (semisweet) chocolate,
   cut into chunks
2 small bananas, mashed

1 Preheat the oven to 200°C/400°F/Gas 6. Arrange 12 paper cases in a muffin tin (pan).

2 In a small bowl, whisk the milk, eggs and melted butter together until the ingredients are thoroughly combined.

3 Sift together the flour and baking powder into a separate bowl. Add the sugar, chocolate and bananas to the flour mixture.

4 Stir gently to combine, gradually stirring in the milk and egg mixture, but do not beat it. Spoon the mixture into the paper cases. Bake for about 20 minutes until the cakes are risen and golden. Allow to stand for 5 minutes, then turn out and leave to cool on a wire rack.

Nutritional information per portion: Energy 303kcal/1268kJ; Protein 4g; Carbohydrate 40g, of which sugars 24.6g; Fat 15.2g, of which saturates 9.3g; Cholesterol 62mg; Calcium 54mg; Fibre 0.8g; Sodium 112mg.

Dark chocolate cupcakes

Ground almonds replace most of the flour in these chocolatey sponge cakes, giving a very rich, deliciously moist result that needs very little adornment: instead of icing, the cakes have been simply finished with a generous dusting of sugar.

MAKES 12

175g/6oz/³⁄₄ cup butter
50g/2oz plain (semisweet) chocolate, broken up
7.5ml/1¹⁄₂ tsp finely grated orange rind
115g/4oz/1 cup ground almonds
115g/4oz/1 cup icing (confectioners')
   sugar, sifted

70g/2¹⁄₂ oz/9 tbsp plain (all-purpose)
   flour, sifted
15ml/1 tbsp unsweetened cocoa powder
6 egg whites

1 Preheat the oven to 190°C/375°F/Gas 5. Grease the cups of a bun tin (pan). Melt the butter with the chocolate and add the orange rind. Set aside to cool slightly.

2 Put the almonds in a large bowl and sift in the icing sugar, flour and cocoa powder.

3 In a separate bowl, beat the egg whites lightly for 15 seconds, just to break them up. Add the egg white to the dry ingredients and mix. Add the melted mixture to the bowl and mix until just combined.

4 Pour the mixture into the bun tin and bake for about 18 minutes, until the cakes are springy to the touch. Leave to cool slightly then turn out on to a wire rack.

5 Dust the cakes with icing sugar to serve, laying a card heart template over each one before dusting. Remove the template carefully.

VARIATION
Decorate the cakes with chocolate hearts. Spread melted chocolate on to a cool surface. Leave until just set, then cut out the shapes. Dust with cocoa and chill. Attach a single heart to the top of each cake with a little sieved jam or icing.

Nutritional information per portion: Energy 255kcal/1063kJ; Protein 4.6g; Carbohydrate 18.1g, of which sugars 13g; Fat 18.8g, of which saturates 9.2g; Cholesterol 34mg; Calcium 42mg; Fibre 1g; Sodium 154mg.

Double chocolate muffins

These jumbo white and plain chocolate muffins are not for everyday eating, so make them to share with friends. Eat fresh from the oven, while the chocolate chunks are still soft and gooey.

MAKES 16 LARGE MUFFINS

400g/14oz/3½ cups plain
   (all-purpose) flour
15ml/1 tbsp baking powder
30ml/2 tbsp unsweetened cocoa powder
115g/4oz/½ cup muscovado
   (molasses) sugar
2 eggs
150ml/¼ pint/⅔ cup sour cream
150ml/¼ pint/⅔ cup milk
60ml/4 tbsp sunflower oil
175g/6oz white chocolate, chopped into
   small pieces
175g/6oz plain (semisweet) chocolate,
   chopped into pieces

1 Preheat the oven to 180°C/350°F/ Gas 4. Lightly grease the cups of a muffin tin (pan).

2 Sift the flour, baking powder and cocoa into a bowl and stir in the sugar. Make a well in the centre.

3 In a separate bowl, beat the eggs with the sour cream, milk and oil, then stir into the well in the dry ingredients. Fold in gently, gradually incorporating all the flour mixture to make a thick and creamy batter.

4 Stir the white and plain chocolate pieces into the batter until the mixture is just combined.

5 Spoon the batter into the greased muffin tin, filling the cups almost to the top. Bake the muffins for 25–30 minutes, until well risen and firm to the touch.

6 Leave to stand in the tin for a few minutes, then serve warm or turn out on to a wire rack to go completely cold.

Nutritional information per portion: Energy 281kcal/1183kJ; Protein 4.7g; Carbohydrate 41.3g, of which sugars 21.9g; Fat 11.9g, of which saturates 5.7g; Cholesterol 7mg; Calcium 94mg; Fibre 1.3g; Sodium 40mg.

Chocolate fairy cakes

These magical little treats are sure to enchant adults and children alike. The chocolate sponge is rich, moist and dark, and contrasts appetizingly with the pure white vanilla-flavoured buttercream.

MAKES 24

175g/6oz/³/4 cup butter, softened
150ml/¹/4 pint/²/3 cup milk
5ml/1 tsp vanilla extract
115g/4oz plain (semisweet) chocolate
15ml/1 tbsp water
275g/10oz/2¹/2 cups plain
   (all-purpose) flour
5ml/1 tsp baking powder
2.5ml/¹/2 tsp bicarbonate of soda
   (baking soda)
300g/11oz/1¹/2 cups caster
   (superfine) sugar
3 eggs

FOR THE VANILLA ICING

40g/1¹/2 oz/3 tbsp butter
115g/4oz/1 cup icing (confectioners') sugar
2.5ml/¹/2 tsp vanilla extract
15–30ml/1–2 tbsp milk

1 Preheat the oven to 180°C/350°F/Gas 4. Arrange 24 paper cases in muffin tins (pans), or grease the cups of the tins.

2 In a large mixing bowl, beat the butter with an electric mixer until it is light and fluffy. Beat in the milk and the vanilla extract.

3 Melt the chocolate with the water in a bowl set over a pan of simmering water, then add to the butter mixture. Sift the flour, baking powder, bicarbonate of soda and sugar over the batter in batches and stir.

4 Add the eggs one at a time, beating well after each addition.

5 Divide the mixture evenly among the muffin cases. Bake for 25 minutes or until a skewer inserted into the centre comes out clean. Cool on a wire rack.

6 For the icing, beat the butter with the icing sugar and vanilla extract. Add enough milk to make a creamy mixture.

7 Spread the icing on top of each of the cooled cakes.

Nutritional information per portion: Energy 210kcal/884kJ; Protein 2.5g; Carbohydrate 30.4g, of which sugars 21.6g; Fat 9.7g, of which saturates 5.8g; Cholesterol 44mg; Calcium 39mg; Fibre 0.5g; Sodium 67mg.

Fruity treats

Whatever your favourite fruit, there is guaranteed to be a cupcake or muffin recipe that incorporates it. Crunchy apples, sharp cranberries, sweet bananas, flavoursome peaches, dried cherries and exotic pineapple are all included in this lavish recipe collection. Try classic Raspberry Muffins or Apple and Calvados Cakes with Quince for a mid-morning treat. Elegant Lemon Meringue Cakes or Fresh Fruit-topped Cupcakes make appealing choices for a more sophisticated occasion.

Blueberry and cinnamon muffins

The traditional blueberry muffin is given a twist with the addition of warming cinnamon. This sweet spice complements the fresh and juicy flavour of the berries.

MAKES 8

115g/4oz/1 cup plain
   (all-purpose) flour
15ml/1 tbsp baking powder
pinch of salt
70g/2½ oz/5 tbsp soft light
   brown sugar
10ml/2 tsp ground cinnamon
1 egg
175ml/6fl oz/¾ cup milk
45ml/3 tbsp vegetable oil
120g/4oz/1 cup blueberries

1 Preheat the oven to 190°C/ 375°F/Gas 5. Line the cups of a muffin tin (pan) with paper cases.

2 Sift the flour, baking powder, salt, sugar and cinnamon into a large mixing bowl. Add the egg, milk and vegetable oil and whisk together until smooth. Fold in the blueberries.

3 Spoon the batter evenly into the muffin cups, filling them about two-thirds full. Bake until a skewer inserted into the centre of a muffin comes out clean, about 25 minutes.

4 Leave to cool in the tin for 10 minutes, then turn out on to a wire rack to go completely cold.

Nutritional information per portion: Energy 141kcal/593kJ; Protein 3.1g; Carbohydrate 21.4g, of which sugars 10.5g; Fat 5.4g, of which saturates 0.9g; Cholesterol 25mg; Calcium 60mg; Fibre 0.9g; Sodium 19mg.

Blueberry and vanilla muffins

Vanilla extract has a sweet aroma and intense, easily identifiable flavour. In this recipe it is used to enhance the natural taste of the juicy blueberries.

MAKES 12

350g/12oz/3 cups plain (all-purpose) flour
10ml/2 tsp baking powder
115g/4oz/½ cup caster (superfine) sugar
2 eggs, beaten
300ml/½ pint/1¼ cups milk
120g/4oz/½ cup butter, melted
5ml/1 tsp vanilla extract
170g/6oz/1½ cups blueberries

1 Preheat the oven to 200°C/400°F/ Gas 6. Line the cups of a muffin tin (pan) with paper cases.

2 Sift the flour and baking powder into a bowl. Stir in the sugar.

3 In another bowl, whisk together the eggs, milk, butter and vanilla.

4 Fold the egg mixture into the dry ingredients with a metal spoon, then gently stir in the blueberries.

5 Spoon the batter into the prepared paper cases, filling them until just below the top. Fill any empty cups half full with water to prevent burning. Bake for 20–25 minutes, until the muffins are well risen and lightly browned.

6 Leave the muffins in the tin for 5 minutes and then turn them out on to a wire rack to cool. Serve warm or cold with a spoonful of berry preserve.

Nutritional information per portion: Energy 243kcal/1021kJ; Protein 4.9g; Carbohydrate 35.9g, of which sugars 13.1g; Fat 9.9g, of which saturates 6g; Cholesterol 56mg; Calcium 82mg; Fibre 1.2g; Sodium 102mg.

Blackberry and almond muffins

Sloe gin and rose water add depth of flavour to these muffins, helping them to stand out from the crowd. Autumnal blackberries are perfectly complemented by the crunch of blanched almonds.

MAKES 12

100g/3½ oz/scant 1 cup fresh blackberries
300g/11oz/2¾ cups plain (all-purpose) flour
50g/2oz/¼ cup soft light brown sugar
20ml/4 tsp baking powder
60g/2¼ oz/⅓ cup blanched almonds, chopped
2 eggs

100ml/3½ fl oz/scant ½ cup milk
50g/2oz/¼ cup butter, melted
15ml/1 tbsp sloe gin
15ml/1 tbsp rose water

1 Preheat the oven to 200°C/400°F/Gas 6. Line the cups of a muffin tin (pan) with paper cases.

2 Rinse the blackberries in a colander and pat dry.

3 Sift the flour, sugar and baking powder into a large bowl.

4 Stir in the almonds and blackberries, mixing them well to coat with the flour mixture. Make a well in the centre of the dry ingredients.

5 In another bowl, whisk the eggs with the milk, then mix in the butter, sloe gin and rose water. Add to the dry ingredients and stir in.

6 Spoon the batter into the prepared paper cases and bake for 20–25 minutes or until golden. Leave to stand for 5 minutes before turning out on to a wire rack to cool. Serve with butter, if you like.

Nutritional information per portion: Energy 181kcal/761kJ; Protein 4.8g; Carbohydrate 25g, of which sugars 5.8g; Fat 7.6g, of which saturates 2.9g; Cholesterol 42mg; Calcium 68mg; Fibre 1.4g; Sodium 49mg.

Raspberry muffins

Wholemeal flour makes these muffins a filling treat to keep hunger pangs at bay and with so little added sugar, they are healthier than most cakes. The raspberries add goodness and flavour.

MAKES 10–12

120g/4oz/1 cup self-raising
   (self-rising) flour
120g/4oz/1 cup self-raising wholemeal
   (self-rising whole-wheat) flour
45ml/3 tbsp caster (superfine) sugar
2 eggs, beaten
200ml/7fl oz/scant 1 cup milk
50g/2oz/¼ cup butter, melted
175g/6oz/1½ cups raspberries, fresh
   or frozen (defrosted for less than
   30 minutes)

1 Preheat the oven to 190°C/375°F/Gas 5. Lightly grease the cups of a muffin tin (pan) or line them with paper cases.

2 Sift the dry ingredients together, then turn in the wholemeal flakes from the sieve (strainer). Make a well in the centre.

3 Beat the eggs, milk and melted butter together in a small bowl until thoroughly combined, then pour into the dry ingredients and mix to a smooth batter.

4 Add the raspberries and gently stir them in. (If you are using frozen raspberries, work quickly so that the cold berries remain solid.) If you mix too much, the raspberries will disintegrate.

5 Spoon the batter into the prepared paper cases. Bake for 30 minutes, until well risen and just firm. Leave to stand, then turn out on to a wire rack. Serve warm or cold. Store in an airtight container for up to 3 days.

Nutritional information per portion: Energy 132kcal/555kJ; Protein 4g; Carbohydrate 19g, of which sugars 5.7g; Fat 5g, of which saturates 2.7g; Cholesterol 42mg; Calcium 48mg; Fibre 1.5g; Sodium 45mg.

Raspberry crumble buns

Make these stylish cakes for a special meal in the summer. For total luxury, serve like scones, with raspberry jam and cream. The nutty crumble topping contrasts beautifully with the soft fruit inside.

MAKES 12

175g/6oz/1½ cups plain
   (all-purpose) flour
10ml/2 tsp baking powder
5ml/1 tsp ground cinnamon
50g/2oz/¼ cup caster (superfine) sugar
50g/2oz/¼ cup soft light brown sugar
115g/4oz/½ cup butter, melted
1 egg
120ml/4fl oz/½ cup milk
225g/8oz/1⅓ cups fresh raspberries
grated rind of 1 lemon

FOR THE CRUMBLE TOPPING
50g/2oz/½ cup pecan nuts,
   finely chopped
50g/2oz/¼ cup soft dark brown sugar
45ml/3 tbsp plain (all-purpose) flour
5ml/1 tsp ground cinnamon
40g/1½ oz/3 tbsp butter, melted

1 Preheat the oven to 180°C/350°F/Gas 4. Arrange 12 paper cases in a muffin tin (pan).

2 Sift the flour, baking powder and cinnamon into a large bowl. Stir in the two kinds of sugar. Make a well in the centre.

3 In another bowl beat together the cooled, melted butter, egg and milk until smooth and light. Pour it into the well in the centre of the flour mixture and stir in gradually until just combined. Stir in the raspberries and lemon rind. Spoon the batter into the muffin cases, filling them almost to the top.

4 To make the crumble topping, mix the pecans, sugar, flour and cinnamon in a large mixing bowl. Stir in the melted butter to create a crumbly texture.

5 Spoon a little of the crumble over the top of each muffin. Bake for about 25 minutes until they are risen and golden. Leave to stand for 5 minutes, then transfer to a wire rack to cool slightly. Serve while still warm.

Nutritional information per portion: Energy 251kcal/1051kJ; Protein 3.4g; Carbohydrate 28.9g, of which sugars 14.9g; Fat 14.4g, of which saturates 7.5g; Cholesterol 46mg; Calcium 56mg; Fibre 1.2g; Sodium 110mg.

Dried apricot muffins

Dried fruits are a handy store-cupboard ingredient, and in this recipe dried apricots are used to flavour these simple tasty muffins, which make the perfect snack at any time of the day. Other dried fruit, such as cherries or cranberries, can also be used.

MAKES 16

450g/1lb/4 cups plain (all-purpose) flour
175g/6oz/³⁄₄ cup butter, diced
30ml/2 tbsp baking powder
pinch of salt
275g/10oz/1¹⁄₃ cups caster (superfine) sugar
75g/3oz/³⁄₄ cup pecans, roughly chopped
rind of 1 large orange, finely grated

50g/2oz/4 tbsp sesame seeds
275g/10oz/1¹⁄₃ cups ready-to-eat dried
    apricots, roughly chopped
4 eggs
400ml/14fl oz/1²⁄₃ cups buttermilk

1 Preheat the oven to 180°C/350°F/Gas 4. Lightly grease the dariole moulds or a slim, tall muffin tin (pan) or line the tin with paper cases.

2 Sift the flour into a large mixing bowl. Add the butter and rub it into the flour to form very fine breadcrumbs.

3 Sift the baking powder, salt and sugar into the flour and butter mixture, then add the pecans, orange rind, sesame seeds and chopped dried apricots. Stir well to combine the ingredients evenly.

4 Mix the eggs with the buttermilk in a jug (pitcher). Add the wet ingredients to the dry ingredients, and stir until just combined.

5 Spoon the batter into the paper cases until almost full and bake for 25 minutes, until a skewer inserted into the centre comes out clean.

6 Leave the muffins to stand and set in the tin for a few minutes before turning out on to a wire rack to go cold.

Nutritional information per portion: Energy 349kcal/1466kJ; Protein 6.9g; Carbohydrate 47.6g, of which sugars 26.1g; Fat 16g, of which saturates 6.9g; Cholesterol 74mg; Calcium 124mg; Fibre 2.4g; Sodium 118mg.

Cranberry and orange muffins

These delicious muffins are perfect to eat at any time of day and are a real energy boost for a mid-morning break. The orange zest adds to the tangy flavour of the cranberries.

MAKES 10

350g/12oz/3 cups plain
   (all-purpose) flour, sifted
15ml/1 tsp baking powder
pinch of salt
115g/4oz/½ cup caster (superfine) sugar
2 eggs
150ml/¼ pint/⅔ cup milk
50ml/2fl oz/¼ cup corn oil
finely grated rind of 1 orange
150g/5oz/1¼ cups cranberries,
   thawed if frozen

1 Preheat the oven to 190°C/375°F/ Gas 5. Lightly grease the cups of a muffin tin (pan) or line them with paper cases.

2 Sift together the flour, baking powder and salt into a large bowl. Add the sugar and stir to mix. Make a well in the centre.

3 Using a fork, lightly beat the eggs with the milk and corn oil in another bowl, until thoroughly combined.

4 Pour the egg mixture into the dry ingredients. Stir with a wooden spoon until just blended to a smooth batter.

5 Gently fold in the orange rind and cranberries with a metal spoon.

6 Fill the paper cases and bake for about 25 minutes, until risen and golden. Leave to stand for 5 minutes before transferring to a wire rack. Serve warm or cold.

Nutritional information per portion: Energy 221kcal/936kJ; Protein 5.1g; Carbohydrate 41.3g, of which sugars 14.6g; Fat 5.1g, of which saturates 1g; Cholesterol 39mg; Calcium 79mg; Fibre 1.3g; Sodium 24mg.

Mandarin syrup cupcakes

For this recipe, mandarins are boiled to soften them and remove some of the bitterness, then puréed to add an intense citrus flavour to the finished cakes, which are then saturated in a citrus syrup.

MAKES 12

3 mandarins
225g/8oz caster (superfine) sugar
6 medium (US large) eggs
225g/8oz ground almonds

FOR THE SYRUP
350g/12oz caster (superfine) sugar
zest of 2 mandarins cut into very
**   fine strips**
juice of ¾ lemon

1 Preheat the oven to 160°C/325°F/ Gas 3. Line a 12-hole muffin tin (pan) with paper cases.

2 Put the whole unpeeled mandarins into a pan and cover generously with boiling water. Bring to the boil, then simmer for about 2 hours. Top up the water level if necessary.

3 Remove the mandarins from the water. When they are cool, split open and remove the pips. Liquidize them into a smooth purée and set aside.

4 Whisk the sugar and eggs until well combined. Stir in the ground almonds and the puréed fruit. Spoon the mixture into the prepared cases and bake for 30 minutes until golden.

5 To make the syrup, dissolve the sugar over a medium heat in 250ml/ 9fl oz water. Add the strips of fruit zest and the lemon juice and bring to the boil. Simmer for 2–3 minutes.

6 Spoon the syrup on to the surface of each of the cakes.

Nutritional information per portion: Energy 344kcal/1449kJ; Protein 7.4g; Carbohydrate 52.2g, of which sugars 51.7g; Fat 13.3g, of which saturates 1.7g; Cholesterol 95mg; Calcium 88mg; Fibre 1.5g; Sodium 41mg.

Orange cupcakes with orange glaze

These delicious cakes are ideal as a snack with a cup of tea or frothy cappuccino. They are finished with a slightly sour orange glaze that perfectly complements the sweetness of the cakes.

MAKES 9–10

75g/3oz/6 tbsp butter
1 egg, lightly beaten
175ml/6fl oz/³/4 cup buttermilk
juice of 1¹/2 Seville (Temple) oranges, plus
grated rind of 2 Seville oranges
225g/8oz/2 cups plain (all-purpose) flour
10ml/2 tsp baking powder
150g/5oz/³/4 cup golden caster
(superfine) sugar
15ml/1 tbsp Seville orange marmalade

FOR THE ORANGE GLAZE
juice and finely grated rind of
¹/2 Seville (Temple) orange
75–90ml/5–6 tbsp icing (confectioners')
sugar, sifted
5ml/1 tsp Seville orange marmalade

1 Preheat the oven to 180°C/350°F/Gas 4. Lightly grease a muffin tin (pan). Melt the butter in a pan over a low heat, set aside to cool slightly.

2 In a bowl mix together the egg, buttermilk, orange juice and grated rind and the cooled, melted butter. Add the flour, baking powder and sugar. Fold in gently, with the marmalade, until just blended.

3 Spoon the mixture into the cups, filling almost to the top. Bake for 25 minutes until golden. Leave to stand then turn on to a wire rack to cool.

4 To make the orange glaze, put the juice in a bowl and beat in the sugar, grated rind and marmalade. The mixture should cover the back of a spoon, but be thin and fluid. Drizzle the glaze in a loose zigzag over the tops of the cakes just before serving.

Nutritional information per portion: Energy 242kcal/1020kJ; Protein 3.5g; Carbohydrate 43.9g, of which sugars 26.8g; Fat 7g, of which saturates 4.3g; Cholesterol 37mg; Calcium 70mg; Fibre 0.7g; Sodium 76mg.

Apricot and maple syrup muffins

Spelt flour has a nutty flavour and is slightly sweet. If you have trouble locating it, substitute plain wholegrain flour instead. Healthy and low in fat, these muffins are ideal for afternoon tea.

MAKES 8 TALL MUFFINS

175g/6oz/²⁄₃ cup dried apricots

40g/1½ oz/3 tbsp caster
   (superfine) sugar

150g/5oz/1¼ cups plain
   (all-purpose) flour

75g/3oz/²⁄₃ cup spelt flour

10ml/2 tsp baking powder

2.5ml/½ tsp bicarbonate of soda
   (baking soda)

120ml/4fl oz/½ cup low-fat natural
   (plain) yogurt

1 egg, lightly beaten

60ml/4 tbsp maple syrup

1 Preheat the oven to 180°C/350°F/Gas 4. Grease and line the dariole moulds with baking parchment.

2 Put the apricots in a pan with 30ml/2 tbsp water and the sugar. Bring slowly to the boil, stirring, then cover and leave to simmer for 4 minutes.

3 Mix the flours, baking powder and bicarbonate of soda in a bowl. Set aside.

4 Drain the apricots, reserving the syrup. Cut the apricots into quarters. In a small bowl, mix the yogurt, egg, maple syrup and reserved syrup and pour them over the dry ingredients. Fold in with the chopped apricot until just combined.

5 Spoon into the lined moulds and bake for 18 minutes. Leave to stand, then transfer to a wire rack to cool completely.

Nutritional information per portion: Energy 216kcal/906kJ; Protein 2.2g; Carbohydrate 32.5g, of which sugars 21.5g; Fat 9.4g, of which saturates 5.7g; Cholesterol 36mg; Calcium 84mg; Fibre 0.7g; Sodium 86mg.

Coconut and rum muffins

Malibu is an intoxicating mix of pineapple juice, coconut milk and white rum. If it's your favourite tipple, then you'll love these muffins, because the same indulgent ingredient combination is used.

MAKES 8

175g/6oz fresh pineapple, plus extra
    for decoration
115g/4oz/½ cup natural glacé
    (candied) cherries, halved, plus
    extra for decoration
45ml/3 tbsp white rum
225g/8oz/2 cups plain (all-purpose) flour
10ml/2 tsp baking powder
175g/6oz/¾ cup butter, softened
175g/6oz/¾ cup soft light brown sugar
2 eggs
7.5ml/1½ tsp vanilla extract
75ml/2½ fl oz/⅓ cup coconut milk
icing (confectioners') sugar, for dusting

1 Cut the pineapple into segments, then into thin slices. Put in a bowl with the glacé cherries. Pour over the rum and leave to marinate for 60 minutes. Preheat the oven to 180°C/350°F/Gas 4. Line the cups of a muffin tin (pan) with paper cases. Sift the flour and the baking powder into a large bowl. Set aside.

2 Beat the butter and sugar until light and creamy, then beat in the eggs, one at a time. Add the vanilla and coconut milk and mix. Add the rum-soaked fruit in small amounts with the flour and baking powder mixture until just combined.

3 Divide the batter between the paper cases and decorate the tops with extra thin pieces of pineapple and cherry halves.

4 Bake for 20–25 minutes until golden on top and springy to touch. Leave to cool slightly then turn out on to a wire rack. Serve warm.

Nutritional information per portion: Energy 420kcal/1764kJ; Protein 4.6g; Carbohydrate 56.9g, of which sugars 35.4g; Fat 19.7g, of which saturates 12.3g; Cholesterol 98mg; Calcium 76mg; Fibre 1.3g; Sodium 197mg.

Dried cherry buns

Sold as a ready-to-eat snack food, dried cherries have a naturally tart flavour. They are a different product to glacé (candied) cherries, which are smothered in syrup.

MAKES 16

250ml/8fl oz/1 cup natural
   (plain) yogurt
225g/8oz/1 cup dried cherries
115g/4oz/½ cup butter, softened
175g/6oz/scant 1 cup caster
   (superfine) sugar
2 eggs
5ml/1 tsp vanilla extract
200g/7oz/1¾ cups plain
   (all-purpose) flour
10ml/2 tsp baking powder
5ml/1 tsp bicarbonate of soda
   (baking soda)

1 In a bowl, combine the yogurt and dried cherries. Cover with clear film (plastic wrap) and leave to stand for 30 minutes until the cherries plump up.

2 Preheat the oven to 180°C/350°F/Gas 4. Lightly grease the cups of a muffin tin (pan) or line them with paper cases.

3 Beat together the butter and caster sugar until light and fluffy. Add the eggs, one at a time, beating well after each addition until fully incorporated. Add the vanilla extract and yogurt and cherry mixture. Stir until thoroughly combined.

4 Sift the flour, baking powder and bicarbonate of soda over the batter in batches. Gently fold in using a metal spoon. Spoon the mixture into the paper cases, filling them two-thirds full. Bake for 20 minutes, until risen and golden. Leave to stand in the tin for 5 minutes, then transfer to a wire rack to cool.

Nutritional information per portion: Energy 187kcal/787kJ; Protein 3.1g; Carbohydrate 29.9g, of which sugars 20.4g; Fat 7g, of which saturates 4g; Cholesterol 39mg; Calcium 63mg; Fibre 0.6g; Sodium 73mg.

Banana and pecan muffins

The rich, buttery flavour of pecan nuts complements the sweetness of banana in these deliciously moreish muffins. Pecans are a healthy treat, and can be stored in the freezer for convenience.

MAKES 8

150g/5oz/1¼ cups plain
    (all-purpose) flour
7.5ml/1½ tsp baking powder
55g/2oz/¼ cup butter, softened
150g/5oz/¾ cup caster (superfine) sugar
1 egg
5ml/1 tsp vanilla extract
3 bananas, mashed
75ml/5 tbsp milk
55g/2oz/⅓ cup pecans, chopped, plus
    extra for decorating (optional)

1 Preheat the oven to 190°C/375°F/ Gas 5. Line the cups of a muffin tin (pan) with paper cases.

2 Sift the flour and baking powder into a small bowl. Set aside.

3 In a large bowl, beat together the butter and sugar until light and fluffy.

4 Add the egg and vanilla to the mixture and beat until smooth. Mix in the mashed bananas.

5 With the mixer on low speed, beat in the flour mixture, alternating it with the milk. Add the pecans.

6 Spoon the batter into the paper cases, filling them two-thirds full. Bake until golden brown and a skewer inserted into the centre comes out clean, 20–25 minutes. Decorate with extra pecans.

7 Cool in the tin for 10 minutes. Transfer to a wire rack to cool for 10 more minutes before serving.

Nutritional information per portion: Energy 277kcal/1164kJ; Protein 4g; Carbohydrate 43.7g, of which sugars 28.5g; Fat 10.7g, of which saturates 4g; Cholesterol 38mg; Calcium 58mg; Fibre 1.3g; Sodium 53mg.

Orange poppy seed muffins

These muffins look attractive baked in large muffin cups and without paper cases so that the poppy seed-flecked sides of the cakes are visible. To serve, split and spread with butter and marmalade.

MAKES 8 LARGE MUFFINS

275g/10oz/2½ cups plain (all-purpose) flour
150g/5oz/¾ cup caster (superfine) sugar
15ml/1 tbsp baking powder
2 eggs
75g/3oz/6 tbsp butter, melted
75ml/5 tbsp vegetable oil
20–25ml/1½ tbsp poppy seeds
30ml/2tbsp orange juice, plus grated rind of 1½ oranges
5ml/1 tsp lemon juice, plus grated rind of 1 lemon

FOR THE ICING

25g/1oz/¼ cup icing (confectioners') sugar
15ml/1 tbsp orange juice

1 Preheat the oven to 180°C/350°F/Gas 4. Lightly grease the cups of a muffin tin (pan) with melted butter or line them with paper cases.

2 Set aside 40g/1½oz of flour. Place the remaining flour with the dry ingredients in a mixing bowl. Make a well in the centre.

3 Mix the eggs, butter, oil, poppy seeds, citrus juices and rinds. Pour over the dry ingredients. Fold in until just mixed. Leave for 1 hour.

4 Fold the reserved flour into the batter but leave it lumpy.

5 Fill the muffin cups three-quarters full. Bake for 25 minutes, until risen and golden. Leave to stand in the tin for a few minutes, then turn out on to a wire rack to go cold.

6 To make the icing, mix the icing sugar and orange juice in a bowl. Add a small quantity of water, if needed, to make a runny consistency. Drizzle over the cakes.

Nutritional information per portion: Energy 377kcal/1583kJ; Protein 5.7g; Carbohydrate 50.7g, of which sugars 24.5g; Fat 18.3g, of which saturates 7.5g; Cholesterol 89mg; Calcium 85mg; Fibre 1.2g; Sodium 107mg.

Passionettes

Moist and moreish, these sweet carrot and apple bakes are guaranteed to be a winner with children and adults alike. They are perfect for autumn eating, with their warming mixed spice.

MAKES 24

150g/5oz/scant ¾ cup butter, melted
200g/7oz/1 cup soft light brown sugar
115g/4oz/1 cup carrots, finely grated
50g/2oz/1 cup dessert apples, peeled and
    finely grated
pinch of salt
1–2 tsp/5–10ml mixed (apple pie) spice
2 eggs
200g/7oz/1¾ cups self-raising
    (self-rising) flour
10ml/2 tsp baking powder
115g/4oz/1 cup walnuts, finely chopped

FOR THE TOPPING

175g/6oz/¾ cup cream cheese
75ml/5 tbsp single (light) cream
50g/2oz/½ cup icing (confectioners') sugar
24 walnut halves
10ml/2 tsp unsweetened cocoa powder

1 Preheat the oven to 180°C/350°F/Gas 4. Arrange 24 paper cases in muffin tins (pans).

2 Put the butter, sugar, carrots, apples, salt, mixed spice and eggs in a mixing bowl and beat well. Sift together the flour and baking powder into the butter and sugar mixture. Add the chopped walnuts and fold in until evenly blended.

3 Fill the paper cases half-full with the batter, then bake for 20–25 minutes, or until a skewer inserted into the centres of the cakes comes out clean. Leave the cakes in the tins for about 5 minutes, before transferring them to a wire rack to cool completely.

4 To make the topping, put the cream cheese in a mixing bowl and beat in the cream and icing sugar until smooth. Put a spoonful of the topping in the centre of each cake, then decorate with the walnuts. Dust with sifted cocoa powder and allow the icing to set before serving.

Nutritional information per portion: Energy 194kcal/808kJ; Protein 3.1g; Carbohydrate 18.3g, of which sugars 11.8g; Fat 12.6g, of which saturates 5.5g; Cholesterol 37mg; Calcium 38mg; Fibre 0.7g; Sodium 75mg.

Pecan and berry muffins

The pecans in these muffins add crunch, while the mixed berries give them a lovely sweet flavour. Use other nuts if you like, such as walnuts, cashews or pistachios.

MAKES 16

450g/1lb/4 cups plain (all-purpose) flour
175g/6oz/³/4 cup butter, diced
30ml/2 tbsp baking powder
pinch of salt
275g/10oz/1¹/3 cups caster
   (superfine) sugar
75g/3oz/³/4 cup pecans,
   roughly chopped
rind of 1 large orange, finely grated
50g/2oz/4 tbsp sesame seeds
275g/10oz/1¹/3 cups dried mixed berries
4 eggs
400ml/14fl oz/1²/3 cups buttermilk

1 Preheat the oven to 180°C/350°F/Gas 4. As a change from paper cases, cut baking parchment into 12.5cm/5in squares and press into the greased cups of a muffin tin (pan).

2 Sift the flour into a large mixing bowl. Add the butter and rub it into the flour to form very fine breadcrumbs. Sift the baking powder, salt and sugar into the flour and butter mixture, then add the pecans, orange rind, sesame seeds and dried mixed berries. Stir well to combine the ingredients evenly.

3 In a jug (pitcher), combine the eggs and the buttermilk, then add to the dry ingredients. Stir until just combined.

4 Spoon the batter into the paper cases until almost full and bake for about 25 minutes, until a skewer inserted into the centre of a muffin comes out clean. Leave the muffins to stand and set in the tin for a few minutes before turning them out on to a wire rack to cool completely.

Nutritional information per portion: Energy 368kcal/1546kJ; Protein 6.6g; Carbohydrate 53g, of which sugars 31.5g; Fat 15.9g, of which saturates 6.9g; Cholesterol 74mg; Calcium 127mg; Fibre 1.7g; Sodium 118mg.

Peach and almond muffins

Ripe peaches with their soft, juicy flesh, velvety coat and distinctive scent are synonymous with late summer. These luxurious fruits make a delightful addition to muffins.

MAKES 8

2 large ripe peaches
225g/8oz/2 cups plain (all-purpose) flour
15ml/1 tbsp baking powder
150g/5oz/¾ cup caster
    (superfine) sugar
40g/1½ oz ground almonds
2 eggs
75g/3oz/6 tbsp butter, melted
50ml/2fl oz/¼ cup sunflower oil
20ml/4 tsp sour cream
15ml/1 tbsp flaked (sliced) almonds,
    for sprinkling
icing (confectioners') sugar, for dusting

1 Preheat the oven to 180°C/350°F/Gas 4. Line the cups of a muffin tin (pan) with paper cases.

2 Cut one peach into small chunks to add to the batter. Cut the other peach into thin crescents and set aside for the topping.

3 Sift the flour, baking powder and sugar into a bowl. Stir in the ground almonds. Form a well in the centre.

4 In a jug (pitcher), whisk together the eggs, melted butter, oil and sour cream until combined. Pour into the dry ingredients and partly fold in. Add the chopped peaches and fold in until just combined.

5 Divide the batter between the paper cases. Decorate the top of each with sliced fruit crescents. Sprinkle over the flaked almonds. Bake for 28 minutes. Leave to stand in the tin for a few minutes, then transfer to a wire rack to cool. Dust with icing sugar.

Nutritional information per portion: Energy 326kcal/1369kJ; Protein 5.7g; Carbohydrate 43.8g, of which sugars 22.2g; Fat 15.5g, of which saturates 6.4g; Cholesterol 71mg; Calcium 74mg; Fibre 1.6g; Sodium 92mg.

Lemon meringue cakes

This recipe is a delightful amalgam of a traditional fairy cake with the classic lemon meringue pie – soft lemon sponge cake is topped with crisp meringue.

MAKES 18

115g/4oz/½ cup butter, softened
200g/7oz/scant 1 cup caster (superfine) sugar
2 eggs
115g/4oz/1 cup self-raising (self-rising) flour
5ml/1 tsp baking powder
grated rind of 2 lemons
30ml/2 tbsp lemon juice
2 egg whites

1 Preheat the oven to 190°C/375°F/Gas 5. Arrange 18 paper cases in muffin tins (pans).

2 Put the butter in a bowl and beat until soft. Add 115g/4oz/generous ½ cup of the caster sugar and continue to beat until the mixture is light and creamy. Add the eggs, one at a time, beating thoroughly after each addition until the mixture is smooth.

3 Sift together the flour and baking powder over the creamed mixture, add half the lemon rind and all the lemon juice and beat well until combined. Divide the mixture among the paper cases, filling each case about two-thirds full.

4 To make the meringue, whisk the egg whites in a clean grease-free bowl until they stand in soft peaks. Stir in the remaining caster sugar and lemon rind.

5 Put a spoonful of the meringue mixture on top of each cake. Cook for 25 minutes, until the meringue is crisp and brown. Serve the cakes warm.

Nutritional information per portion: Energy 123kcal/514kJ; Protein 1.7g; Carbohydrate 16.6g, of which sugars 11.7g; Fat 6g, of which saturates 3.5g; Cholesterol 35mg; Calcium 19mg; Fibre 0.2g; Sodium 54mg.

Lemon and elderflower poppy seed muffins

Poppy seeds add an unexpectedly light and crunchy texture to the cake crumb in these muffins, which are traditionally soaked in a sweet lemon syrup.

MAKES 8 TALL MUFFINS

225g/8oz/2 cups self-raising (self-rising) flour
200g/7oz/1 cup caster (superfine) sugar
40g/1¹/₂ oz ground almonds
2 eggs, beaten
75g/3oz/6 tbsp butter, melted
50ml/2fl oz/¹/₄ cup vegetable oil
25ml/1¹/₂ tbsp poppy seeds
30ml/2 tbsp lemon juice
grated rind of 1 lemon
grated rind of 1 clementine

FOR THE SYRUP

115g/4oz/generous ¹/₂ cup caster
   (superfine) sugar
50ml/2fl oz /¹/₄ cup lemon juice
15ml/1 tbsp elderflower cordial
lemon segments, to decorate

1 Preheat the oven to 180°C/350°F/Gas 4. Grease and line 8 dariole moulds with baking parchment.

2 Sift the flour and sugar into a large bowl. Stir in the ground almonds. Make a well in the centre.

3 In a jug (pitcher) mix together the eggs, butter, oil, poppy seeds, lemon juice and the grated fruit rinds. Pour the liquid into the flour mix and stir until just combined.

4 Fill the lined moulds three-quarters full and bake for 25 minutes. Leave to stand for a few minutes, then transfer to a wire rack to go cold.

5 To make the syrup, put the sugar, 120ml/4fl oz/¹/₂ cup water and the lemon juice in a pan and heat gently, stirring frequently until dissolved.

6 Leave to boil without stirring for 5–6 minutes until syrupy. Remove from the heat. Stir in the cordial. Prick holes in the top of each muffin using a skewer. Pour over the warm syrup. Decorate the muffin tops with thin segments of lemon, before serving.

Nutritional information per portion: Energy 408kcal/1717kJ; Protein 5.9g; Carbohydrate 63.9g, of which sugars 42.4g; Fat 16.1g, of which saturates 6.2g; Cholesterol 69mg; Calcium 94mg; Fibre 1.4g; Sodium 92mg.

Apple and sour cream crumble muffins

Two-thirds of the cooking apples in this recipe are chopped and baked in the muffin batter.
The remaining apples are sliced and coated in an almond crumble, which makes a crunchy topping.

MAKES 8

3 small cooking apples, peeled and cored
10ml/2 tsp caster (superfine) sugar,
    for coating
5ml/1 tsp ground cinnamon
250g/9oz/2¼ cups plain (all-purpose) flour
15ml/1 tbsp baking powder
115g/4oz/½ cup caster sugar
75g/3oz/6 tbsp butter, melted
2 eggs, beaten
30ml/2 tbsp sour cream

FOR THE CINNAMON CRUMBLE

30ml/2 tbsp plain (all-purpose) flour
45ml/3 tbsp demerara (raw) sugar
30ml/2 tbsp ground almonds
pinch of ground cinnamon

1 Preheat the oven to 190°C/375°F/Gas 5. Line the cups of a muffin tin (pan) with paper cases.

2 To make the crumble, place all the crumble ingredients together in a large bowl and mix. Cut one of the apples into thin crescents, and toss the pieces in the crumble, so that they are covered. Set aside.

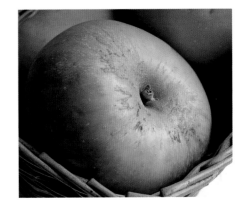

3 Dice the remaining apples. Sift 10ml/2 tsp sugar and the cinnamon over the top. Set aside.

4 Sift the flour, baking powder and sugar into a bowl. Stir in the melted butter, eggs and sour cream.

5 Add the apple chunks and lightly fold them into the batter. Fill the paper cases with the batter, then arrange the crumble-coated apple pieces on top.

6 Bake the muffins for 25 minutes until they are risen and golden brown. Allow to cool on a wire rack before serving.

Nutritional information per portion: Energy 272kcal/1144kJ; Protein 4.8g; Carbohydrate 42.8g, of which sugars 19g; Fat 10.2g, of which saturates 6g; Cholesterol 71mg; Calcium 65mg; Fibre 1.6g; Sodium 92mg.

Apple and Calvados cakes with quince

The subtle bouquet of Calvados (Normandy apple brandy) and the earthy, fruity flavour of quince add depth to simple apple cakes. Quince paste is always available, but when the fruit is in season replace a third of the chopped apple with finely grated fresh quince to add extra flavour.

MAKES 10

250g/9oz cooking apple, peeled and cored
45ml/3 tbsp quince paste
75g/3oz/6 tbsp butter, melted
15ml/1 tbsp Calvados
225g/8oz/2 cups plain (all-purpose) flour
10ml/2 tsp baking powder
75g/3oz/⅓ cup caster (superfine) sugar
1 egg, lightly beaten

60ml/4 tbsp buttermilk
grated rind of 1 lemon

FOR THE QUINCE GLAZE
45ml/3 tbsp quince or apple jelly
15ml/1 tbsp water
5ml/1 tsp lemon juice
30ml/2 tbsp Calvados

1 Preheat the oven to 180°C/350°F/Gas 4. Grease the cups of a large muffin tin (pan) or line them with paper muffin cases.

2 Slice one quarter of the apple very thinly and reserve in a bowl of water acidulated with a squeeze of lemon. Roughly dice the rest of the apple and set aside in another bowl of acidulated water.

3 In a small pan, gently melt the quince paste with the butter over a low heat, mashing the paste with a wooden spoon to break up any little lumps. Remove the pan from the heat. Stir in the Calvados and set aside.

4 Sift the dry ingredients into a large bowl. In another bowl, stir the egg and the buttermilk together and add the grated lemon rind.

5 Pour the egg mixture into the dry ingredients, with the butter, quince paste and Calvados and the chopped apple. Stir until just combined, then spoon into the prepared muffin tin.

6 Press a few slices of apple into the top of each cake. Bake for 25–30 minutes until golden.

7 To make the glaze, put the jelly, water and lemon juice in a small pan, and boil rapidly until slightly thickened. Add the Calvados and simmer for about 1 minute. Brush over the muffins while still warm.

Nutritional information per portion: Energy 318kcal/1327kJ; Protein 8g; Carbohydrate 23.6g, of which sugars 6.9g; Fat 22g, of which saturates 11g; Cholesterol 85mg; Calcium 124mg; Fibre 1g; Sodium 491mg.

Apple crisp muffins

Caramelized oven-dried fruit slices add a natural and appealing decoration to fresh fruit muffins. These apple muffins are topped with slices of apple, but you could use pears, too.

MAKES 6

1 egg, beaten
40g/1½ oz/3 tbsp caster (superfine) sugar
120ml/4fl oz/½ cup milk
50g/2oz/¼ cup butter, melted
150g/5oz/1¼ cups plain (all-purpose) flour
7.5ml/1½ tsp baking powder
2.5ml/½ tsp mixed (apple pie) spice
2 small eating apples, peeled, cored and
    finely chopped

FOR THE APPLE CRISPS

1–1½ small ripe apples, unpeeled and
    thinly sliced
60g/2oz/generous ¼ cup caster
    (superfine) sugar

1 First make the apple crisps. Line a baking sheet with parchment. Preheat the oven to 120°C/250°F/Gas ½. Arrange the apple slices between sheets of kitchen paper to drain off their juices.

2 Put the sugar and 50ml/2 oz/¼ cup water in a pan. Heat until the sugar dissolves and bring slowly to the boil. Leave to boil for 3 minutes, then remove from the heat.

3 Pour the syrup into a bowl and immerse the fruit in it for about 3 minutes. Remove the fruit (reserving the syrup) and spread out the slices over the baking sheet. Bake for 2 hours until they shrink and turn crisp. Leave to dry over a wire rack.

4 To make the muffins, preheat the oven to 200°C/400°F/Gas 6. Line the cups of a muffin tin (pan) with paper cases.

5 Mix the egg, sugar, milk and melted butter in a large bowl. Sift in the flour, baking powder and mixed (apple pie) spice. Add the chopped apples and mix roughly. Spoon the mixture into the prepared paper cases.

6 Brush the apple crisps with the reserved cooking syrup and place one on top of each muffin. Bake for 30 minutes, until and golden. Leave to stand for 5 minutes before transferring to a wire rack to cool.

Nutritional information per portion: Energy 243kcal/1026kJ; Protein 4.3g; Carbohydrate 40.9g, of which sugars 21.9g; Fat 8.2g, of which saturates 4.8g; Cholesterol 52mg; Calcium 75mg; Fibre 1.3g; Sodium 87mg.

Fresh raspberry and fig cakes

Beautiful purple figs, with their luscious red flesh, nestle with fresh raspberries in this delicious cake batter, which puffs up around them in a golden dome as it bakes.

MAKES 8–9

140g/5oz/³⁄₄ cup fresh raspberries
15ml/1 tbsp caster (superfine) sugar
3 fresh figs
225g/8oz/2 cups plain (all-purpose) flour
10ml/2 tsp baking powder
140g/5oz/³⁄₄ cup golden caster
   (superfine) sugar
85g/3¹⁄₂oz/7 tbsp butter, melted
1 egg, beaten
285ml/¹⁄₂ pint buttermilk
grated rind of ¹⁄₂ small orange

1 Preheat the oven to 180°C/350°F/Gas 4. Grease the cups of a large muffin tin (pan) or line with paper muffin cases.

2 Arrange the raspberries in one layer on a plate and sprinkle with the 15ml/ 1 tbsp caster sugar. Slice the figs vertically into eighths and set aside.

3 Sift the flour and baking powder into a large mixing bowl and mix in the sugar. Make a well in the centre of the dry ingredients.

4 In another bowl, mix the cooled melted butter with the egg, buttermilk and orange rind. Pour into the dry ingredients and fold in until just blended.

5 Set aside a small quantity of the raspberries and figs. Sprinkle the remaining fruit over the surface of the batter and fold in lightly. Spoon the mixture into the tin or the paper cases, filling each not more than two-thirds full.

6 Lightly press the reserved fruit into the top of the batter. Bake for 25 minutes until risen and golden. Leave in the tin for 5 minutes, then cool on a wire rack.

Nutritional information per portion: Energy 260kcal/1098kJ; Protein 4.7g; Carbohydrate 43.2g, of which sugars 24.2g; Fat 8.9g, of which saturates 5.4g; Cholesterol 44mg; Calcium 107mg; Fibre 1.7g; Sodium 102mg.

Pear muffin for two

In this recipe, the muffin mixture is baked in a larger cake tin, but you could also make regular-sized muffins. The pear is used both for flavouring and for decoration.

MAKES 1 LARGE MUFFIN

225g/8 oz/2 cups plain
   (all-purpose) flour
90g/3½ oz/½ cup butter, diced
15ml/1 tbsp baking powder
pinch of salt
150g/5oz/⅔ cups caster
   (superfine) sugar
1 pear, peeled, halved and cored
75g/3oz/¾ cup pecans, roughly chopped
rind of 1 large orange, finely grated
50g/2oz/4 tbsp sesame seeds
2 eggs
200ml/7fl oz/scant 1 cup buttermilk

1 Preheat the oven to 180°C/350°F/Gas 4. Line and grease a 12.5cm/5in cake tin (pan).

2 Sift the flour into a large mixing bowl. Add the butter and rub it into the flour to form fine breadcrumbs.

3 Sift the baking powder, salt and sugar into the flour and butter mixture. Chop one half of the pear, then add to the dry ingredients with the pecans, orange rind and sesame seeds. Stir well to combine evenly.

4 Combine the eggs and buttermilk in a jug (pitcher) and add to the dry ingredients. Stir until just combined. Spoon the batter into the cake tin, and place the remaining pear half on top.

5 Bake for 25 minutes, until a skewer inserted into the centre comes out clean. Leave to stand in the tin for a few minutes before cooling on a wire rack.

Nutritional information per portion: Energy 194kcal/814kJ; Protein 3.6g; Carbohydrate 22.6g, of which sugars 11.8g; Fat 10.6g, of which saturates 3.8g; Cholesterol 37mg; Calcium 69mg; Fibre 1.1g; Sodium 60mg.

Citrus syrup cupcakes

These moist, syrupy cakes, with a very intense tangy citrus flavour, are made without flour, which makes them safe to eat for anyone who has a wheat allergy. To make a luscious dessert add your choice of berries and a scoop of vanilla ice cream.

MAKES 12

3 clementines
6 eggs
225g/8oz/1 cup caster (superfine) sugar
225g/8oz/2 cups ground almonds
icing (confectioners') sugar, to dust

FOR THE CITRUS SYRUP
350g/12oz/3 cups caster
   (superfine) sugar
rind of 1 clementine, pith removed, cut
   into very fine strips
juice of ¾ lemon

1 Put the whole, unpeeled clementines into a pan and cover generously with boiling water. Bring to the boil, then simmer for about 2 hours. This will soften the fruit and remove some of the bitterness from the skin. Keep a check on the water level and top up as necessary with boiling water.

2 Meanwhile, preheat the oven to 160°C/325°F/Gas 3. Set 12 oblong silicone cake cases on a baking sheet, or line a 12-hole bun tin (pan) with paper cake cases.

3 Remove the fruit from the water and leave to cool. Split open and discard the pips (seeds). Liquidize the fruit into a purée. Set aside.

4 Whisk the eggs and sugar together until foamy, then stir in the ground almonds and the fruit purée. Pour the mixture into the prepared cases and bake for 30 minutes.

5 To make the citrus syrup, dissolve the sugar in 250ml/9fl oz water over a medium heat. Add the strips of rind and the lemon juice and bring to the boil. Reduce the heat and simmer for 2–3 minutes, until the liquid coats the back of a spoon.

6 Allow the cakes to cool in the cases, then drizzle the warm syrup over, a spoonful at a time.

Nutritional information per portion: Energy 344kcal/1449kJ; Protein 7.4g; Carbohydrate 52.2g, of which sugars 51.7g; Fat 13.3g, of which saturates 1.7g; Cholesterol 95mg; Calcium 88mg; Fibre 1.5g; Sodium 41mg.

Raspberry crunch friands

Egg whites are combined with ground nuts, melted butter and very little flour. The raw mixture has quite a loose consistency, but as they bake they will become just as firm as other cakes.

MAKES 12

115g/4oz/1 cup ground almonds
225g/8oz/2 cups icing (confectioners')
 sugar, sifted
70g/2½ oz/9 tbsp plain (all-purpose)
 flour, sifted
6 egg whites
175g/6oz/¾ cup butter, melted
115g/4oz/¾ cup fresh raspberries

FOR THE CRUNCHY SUGAR FROSTING
juice of 1 small lemon
150g/5oz/¾ cup caster (superfine) sugar
very finely cut strips of candied lemon
 rind (optional)

1 Preheat the oven to 200°C/400°F/Gas 6. Grease the cups of a friand or bun tin (pan) and dust lightly with flour. Turn the tin upside down and tap it sharply on the work surface to get rid of any excess flour.

2 Mix the ground almonds, sugar and flour. In a separate bowl, beat the egg whites lightly for 15 seconds, or just enough to break them up. Add the egg whites to the dry ingredients and mix. Add the melted butter to the bowl and mix until just combined.

3 Pour the mixture into the cups and press one raspberry into each one. Bake for 25 minutes until the friands are pale golden and springy to the touch. Leave to cool slightly, then turn them out on to a wire rack.

4 To make the sugar frosting, mix the lemon juice with the sugar and set aside for 10 minutes for the sugar to partly dissolve. Drizzle over the tops of the cooled cakes and leave to set for several hours. Top with a few curls of candied lemon rind, if you like.

Nutritional information per portion: Energy 317kcal/1330kJ; Protein 4.4g; Carbohydrate 38.3g, of which sugars 33.6g; Fat 17.4g, of which saturates 8.4g; Cholesterol 34mg; Calcium 53mg; Fibre 1.1g; Sodium 143mg.

Fresh fruit-topped cupcakes

Use summer fruits and a dusting of icing sugar to dress up basic cupcakes. This luxurious way to serve them means they'll go down well with adults as well as children.

MAKES 8–9

175g/6oz/³⁄₄ cup butter, softened
175g/6oz/³⁄₄ cup caster (superfine) sugar
5ml/1 tsp vanilla extract, or 5ml/
    1 tsp finely grated lemon rind
4 eggs, lightly beaten
175g/6oz/1¹⁄₂ cups self-raising
    (self-rising) flour, sifted

FOR THE TOPPING

400ml/14fl oz/1²⁄₃ cups whipping cream
275g/10 oz mixed berries
icing (confectioners') sugar, for dusting

1 Preheat the oven to 180°C/350°F/Gas 4. Line 8–9 cups of a bun tin (pan) with paper cases. Place the butter and sugar in a mixing bowl.

2 Beat together until light and creamy. Add the vanilla or lemon rind. Gradually add the eggs, beating after each addition. Add the flour and fold into the mixture until just combined.

3 Divide the mixture among the paper cases and bake for 20 minutes until golden brown and the centres feel firm to the touch.

4 Remove from the oven. Leave to cool for 5 minutes, then turn the cakes out on to a wire rack to cool completely before decorating.

5 Scoop out a circle of sponge from the top of the cakes using a small sharp knife. Set the lids to one side. Whip the cream until stiff peaks form. Place a spoonful of cream in each sponge and top with fruit. Replace the lids at an angle and dust with icing sugar.

Nutritional information per portion: Energy 536kcal/2253kJ; Protein 5.6g; Carbohydrate 78.4g, of which sugars 74.9g; Fat 24.4g, of which saturates 11.4g; Cholesterol 107mg; Calcium 87mg; Fibre 1.1g; Sodium 171mg.

Sweet and indulgent

Scrumptious cupcakes and muffins, packed with luxurious ingredients and iced with decadent frostings, are a pleasure intended for sharing. Try Banoffee Muffins with Caramel or rich and fruity Chocolate and Sour Cherry Cakes. Madeleine Cakes with Raspberry Buttercream are served with gorgeous mini madeleines, while Carrot Cupcakes topped with creamy icing and marzipan carrots are perfect for every sweet tooth.

Simple iced cupcakes

These no-fuss cupcakes are perfect for a children's party, and the recipe is easy enough for the children to help you make them. The simple glacé icing is mixed with lemon juice for a tangy flavour.

MAKES 12

115g/4oz/1 cup self-raising
   (self-rising) flour
2.5ml/½ tsp baking powder
115g/4oz/½ cup butter, softened
115g/4oz/½ cup caster (superfine) sugar
2 eggs
5ml/1 tsp lemon juice

FOR THE LEMON ICING

175g/6oz/1½ cups icing
   (confectioners') sugar
30ml/2 tbsp lemon juice
5ml/1 tsp hot water
food colouring, optional

1 Preheat the oven to 180°C/350°F/Gas 4. Line a 12-cup bun tin (pan) with paper cases. Sift the flour with the baking powder and set aside.

2 In a large mixing bowl, beat the butter and sugar together using an electric mixer until light and fluffy. Add the eggs a little at a time, beating the mixture well after each addition. Gently fold in the sifted flour using a metal spoon. Add the lemon juice and stir to blend.

3 Fill the prepared cups half full. Bake for 13–15 minutes until the cakes look golden and the tops spring back when touched. Transfer to a wire rack to cool.

4 To make the icing, sift the icing sugar and gradually mix in the lemon juice and water until the mixture is smooth. Add a little food colouring, if you want. Spoon a little icing on to each cake and smooth level with a spatula.

Nutritional information per portion: Energy 211kcal/887kJ; Protein 2.1g; Carbohydrate 32.7g, of which sugars 25.4g; Fat 8.9g, of which saturates 5.5g; Cholesterol 54mg; Calcium 32mg; Fibre 0.3g; Sodium 85mg.

Sugar sparkle cupcakes

These delicately rose-flavoured cakes are pretty in pink and perfect for a girls-only party.
Have fun decorating them with sugar sprinkles, sugar flowers or shapes in your choice of colours.

MAKES 12

115g/4oz/1 cup self-raising
   (self-rising) flour
115g/4oz/generous ½ cup caster
   (superfine) sugar
115g/4oz/½ cup unsalted
   butter, softened
2 eggs
15ml/1 tbsp rose water
15ml/1 tbsp milk
pink food colouring, optional

FOR THE TOPPING AND
DECORATION
225g/8oz/2 cups icing (confectioners')
   sugar, sifted
15ml/1 tbsp rose water
pink sugar sprinkles, or sugar flowers
   or shapes

1 Preheat the oven to 190°C/375°F/Gas 5. Line a 12-cup muffin tray with paper cases.

2 Put the flour, sugar, butter and eggs into a large bowl with the rose water and beat until smooth. Add the milk and a few drops of pink food colour. Divide among the paper cases.

3 Bake for 15–20 minutes, or until the cakes are risen and golden, and are just firm to the touch. Remove from the tray and put on a wire rack to cool.

4 To make the topping, sift the icing sugar into a bowl and add the rose water with a few drops of pink food colouring and 5ml/1 tsp cold water, or enough to mix to a spreadable icing.

5 Spoon a little icing over the cakes, then top with sprinkles, flowers or shapes.

Nutritional information per portion: Energy 249kcal/1041kJ; Protein 2.4g; Carbohydrate 27g, of which sugars 20.4g; Fat 16.5g, of which saturates 9.5g; Cholesterol 76mg; Calcium 35mg; Fibre 0.3g; Sodium 89mg.

Marshmallow daisy cakes

These lemony cakes are as fresh as a daisy, and they are quick and so very simple to make and bake. The marshmallow flowers take moments to create – all you need is a pair of scissors.

MAKES 12

115g/4oz/1 cup self-raising
   (self-rising) flour
5ml/1 tsp baking powder
115g/4oz/generous ½ cup caster
   (superfine) sugar
115g/4oz/½ cup soft tub margarine
2 eggs, beaten
15ml/1 tbsp lemon juice
finely grated rind of 1 lemon

FOR THE DECORATION
buttercream
12 pink and white marshmallows
caster (superfine) sugar, for dusting
small sweets (candies)

1 Preheat the oven to 180°C/350°F/Gas 4. Line a 12-cup muffin tin (pan) with paper cases.

2 Sift the flour, baking powder and sugar into a large bowl, then add the remaining ingredients. Beat until light and creamy, then place heaped spoonfuls into the paper cases.

3 Bake for about 20 minutes, or until golden and firm to the touch. Allow to cool for 2 minutes, then turn out on to a wire rack to go cold.

4 When cold, spread the top of each cake with a little buttercream. Use kitchen scissors to cut each marshmallow to make 4 half-moon shapes. Dip the cut marshmallow edges in caster sugar to prevent sticking.

5 Press the tips of four marshmallow halves together to form a flower. Arrange them on top of a cupcake and press a small sweet into the centre.

Nutritional information per portion: Energy 115kcal/483kJ; Protein 1.3g; Carbohydrate 16.5g, of which sugars 12.1g; Fat 5.4g, of which saturates 3.2g; Cholesterol 31mg; Calcium 18mg; Fibre 0.2g; Sodium 43mg.

Lemon cupcakes with citrus crème fraîche

Add a zing to the afternoon break with the freshly baked aromas of lemon and cardamom – the signature ingredients in these delicious cupcakes.

MAKES 8–9

225g/8oz/2 cups plain (all-purpose) flour
10ml/2 tsp baking powder
150g/5oz/³/₄ cup caster (superfine)
 sugar, or 75ml/5 tbsp clear honey
1 egg, beaten
300ml/¹/₂ pint/1¹/₄ cups natural
 (plain) yogurt
15ml/1 tbsp freshly grated lemon rind
75g/3oz/6 tbsp butter, melted
8 cardamom seeds crushed to a powder

**FOR THE FROSTING AND
DECORATION**
225g/8oz/1 cup crème fraîche
50g/2oz/¹/₂ cup icing (confectioners')
 sugar, double sifted, plus extra
 for dusting
juice of 1 lemon
finely grated rind of 2 lemons
small quantity of sugarpaste
paste food colouring

1 Preheat the oven to 180°C/350°F/Gas 4. Line the cups of a bun tin (pan) with paper cases. Sift the flour and baking powder into a large bowl and stir in the sugar (but not the honey, if using).

2 In another bowl mix together the egg, yogurt, lemon rind, honey (if using) and melted butter. Add to the dry ingredients with the ground cardamom and fold lightly together. Spoon the mixture into the cases, filling them two-thirds full. Bake for 25 minutes until springy. Leave to cool on a wire rack.

3 For the frosting, whisk the crème fraîche, sugar, lemon juice and rind together until thick and creamy. Cover and chill for at least an hour, then spread a little frosting over each cake.

4 Tint the sugarpaste to the desired colour. Roll out to a thickness of 3mm/ ¹/₈ in on a work surface dusted with sifted icing sugar and stamp a flower for each cake. Press a small ball of paste into each centre and shape the petals gently. Press a flower into the top of each cake.

Nutritional information per portion: Energy 238kcal/1004kJ; Protein 4.8g; Carbohydrate 39.2g, of which sugars 20.2g; Fat 8.1g, of which saturates 4.9g; Cholesterol 41mg; Calcium 108mg; Fibre 0.8g; Sodium 98mg.

Vanilla butterfly cakes

These pretty little cakes are filled with a simple vanilla buttercream. The butterfly 'wings' are so easy to make, but when dusted with a little icing sugar make a really elegant decoration.

MAKES 10

175g/6oz/¾ cup butter, softened
175g/6oz/¾ cup caster (superfine) sugar
5ml/1 tsp vanilla extract
4 eggs, lightly beaten
175g/6oz/1½ cups self-raising
    (self-rising) flour, sifted

FOR THE FILLING

75g/3oz/6 tbsp butter, softened
175g/6oz/1½ cups icing (confectioners') sugar,
    double sifted, plus extra for dusting
½ vanilla pod (bean), split, or a few drops
    of vanilla extract

1 Preheat the oven to 180°C/350°F/Gas 4. Line 8–9 cups of a bun tin (pan) with paper cases.

2 Beat the butter and sugar together until light and creamy. Add the vanilla. Gradually add the eggs, beating well after each addition. Add the sifted flour and fold into the mixture until just combined.

3 Divide the mixture among the paper cases and bake for 20 minutes until the cakes are golden brown and the centres feel firm to the touch. Remove from the oven. Leave to cool in the tin for 5 minutes, then turn out on to a wire rack to cool completely.

4 To make the buttercream filling, beat the butter and icing sugar together until smooth. For the best vanilla flavour, split the vanilla pod in half and scrape out the seeds. Discard the pod and mix the seeds into the buttercream. Alternatively, add a few drops of vanilla extract to the mixture.

5 When the cakes have cooled, carefully cut round the lightly domed tops with a small sharp knife and remove the top of each cake. Slice the tops in half to form two semicircles, to make the butterfly wings. Set aside.

6 Use a piping (icing) bag with a star nozzle to pipe a whirl of buttercream into each cake. Press the wings into the cream and dust with sifted icing sugar.

Nutritional information per portion: Energy 455kcal/1905kJ; Protein 4.8g; Carbohydrate 55.3g, of which sugars 40.9g; Fat 25.4g, of which saturates 15.7g; Cholesterol 148mg; Calcium 106mg; Fibre 0.6g; Sodium 312mg.

Ginger cupcakes with lemon glacé icing

Cool lemon icing offsets the warm ginger flavour of these delicious little cakes, which are charmingly decorated with small 'gingerbread' figures cut out of spiced marzipan.

MAKES 12–14

175g/6oz/¾ cup butter, softened

175g/6oz/¾ cup golden caster
   (superfine) sugar

3 eggs, lightly beaten

25ml/1½ tbsp black treacle (molasses)

35ml/2½ tbsp syrup from a jar of
   preserved ginger

225g/8oz/2 cups self-raising (self-rising)
   flour, sifted

10ml/2 tsp ground ginger

25ml/1½ tbsp ground almonds

30ml/2 tbsp single (light) cream

**FOR THE ICING AND
DECORATION**

350g/12oz/3 cups icing
   (confectioners') sugar

60ml/4 tbsp lemon juice

10ml/2 tsp water

115g/4oz golden marzipan

2.5ml/½ tsp mixed (pumpkin pie) spice

a few drops ginger-brown food colouring

1 Preheat the oven to 180°C/350°F/Gas 4. Line the cups of a large bun tin (pan) with paper cases.

2 Beat the butter and sugar together until light and creamy. Gradually beat in the eggs in batches, beating well between each addition. Fold in the black treacle and the ginger syrup.

3 Sift in the flour with the ground ginger and fold in lightly. Add the ground almonds, then the cream, and stir until well combined. Half-fill the prepared cups and bake for 20 minutes, or until slightly springy to the touch. Leave for a few minutes. Turn out on to a wire rack and cool completely.

4 To make the icing, sift the icing (confectioners') sugar into a bowl and gradually mix in the lemon juice until the mixture is smooth, adding the water if necessary to get the correct consistency.

5 Spoon the icing on to each cake and smooth. For the gingerbread figures, knead the ground spice and food colouring into the marzipan and roll out thinly. Using a small cutter, cut out the shapes and stick them to the cakes.

Nutritional information per portion: Energy 314kcal/1320kJ; Protein 3.9g; Carbohydrate 45.6g, of which sugars 33.3g; Fat 14.1g, of which saturates 7.6g; Cholesterol 71mg; Calcium 64mg; Fibre 0.8g; Sodium 115mg.

Soft cheese cupcakes

Although cupcakes are very popular nowadays, it's unusual to come across one with a mild goat's cheese flavour. A fresh flower decoration looks lovely.

MAKES 12

140g/5oz/²/₃ cup butter, softened
185g/6¹/₂ oz/³/₄ cup caster
    (superfine) sugar
3 eggs
15ml/1 tbsp grated lemon rind
140g/5oz/²/₃ cup soft goat's cheese
45ml/3 tbsp mixed (candied)
    peel, chopped
20ml/4 tsp buttermilk
200g/7oz/1³/₄ cups self-raising
    (self-rising) flour

FOR THE FROSTING

450g/1lb/2 cups soft goat's cheese
300g/11oz/2³/₄ cups icing
    (confectioners') sugar, sifted
fresh edible flowers such as violets or
    pansies, to decorate

1 Preheat the oven to 180°C/350°F/Gas 4. Line the cups of a bun tin (pan) with paper cases.

2 Beat the butter and caster sugar together until light and creamy. Gradually beat in the eggs, one at a time, beating well after each addition.

3 Beat in the lemon rind, goat's cheese, mixed peel and buttermilk. Lightly fold in the flour. Spoon the cake mixture into the prepared cups and lightly smooth it level.

4 Bake for 25 minutes, or until the centre of each cake is firm and slightly springy to the touch. Leave to cool slightly, then turn out on to a wire rack to cool completely.

5 To make the frosting, soften the goat's cheese by beating it in a large mixing bowl. Stir in the sifted icing sugar until combined. Spread a little of the frosting on top of each of the cooled cakes and decorate with the fresh edible flowers.

Nutritional information per portion: Energy 487kcal/2044kJ; Protein 13.8g; Carbohydrate 58g, of which sugars 45.3g; Fat 23.9g, of which saturates 15.5g; Cholesterol 120mg; Calcium 126mg; Fibre 0.7g; Sodium 415mg.

Banoffee muffins with caramel

Banoffee pie was invented in the 1980s and immediately became famous. It's a sweet confection that uses dulce de leche, made by boiling cans of condensed milk for several hours.

MAKES 8–9

75g/3oz/6 tbsp butter, softened
115g/4oz/generous ½ cup soft light
　　brown sugar
1 egg, lightly beaten
225g/8oz/2 cups self-raising
　　(self-rising) flour
12.5ml/2½ tsp baking powder
2 large bananas
rind of 1 orange, finely grated
rind of ½ lemon, finely grated
30ml/2 tbsp buttermilk or sour cream
45ml/3 tbsp dulce de leche

FOR THE FROSTING

2.5ml/½ tsp instant coffee granules,
　　dissolved in 5ml/1 tsp hot water
150ml/¼ pint/⅔ cup double
　　(heavy) cream
7.5ml/1½ tsp dulce de leche
½ banana, sliced into 18 discs

FOR THE TOFFEE SYRUP

10ml/2 tsp dark muscovado
　　(molasses) sugar
30ml/2 tbsp dulce
　　de leche

1 Preheat the oven to 190°C/375°F/ Gas 5. Lightly grease the cups of a muffin tin (pan).

2 Beat the butter and sugar until creamy. Gradually add the egg.

3 Sift the flour and baking powder into a separate bowl and set aside.

4 Mash the bananas and fold half into the butter–sugar mixture. Add the grated rinds and half of the flour. Fold in the remaining flour and bananas with the buttermilk or sour cream, until just combined.

5 Spoon the batter into the muffin cups until three-quarters full. Bake for 20 minutes until golden and springy. Stand for 5 minutes, then cool completely on a wire rack. Make a cavity in the top of each muffin. Fill with dulce de leche.

6 To make the frosting, beat together the coffee, cream and dulce de leche and beat well. Spread over the cakes. Top with the banana slices.

7 For the syrup, dissolve the sugar in 5ml/1 tsp boiling water. Add the dulce de leche. Drizzle over the cakes.

Nutritional information per portion: Energy 341kcal/1432kJ; Protein 4g; Carbohydrate 45.5g, of which sugars 26g; Fat 18.1g, of which saturates 10.6g; Cholesterol 82mg; Calcium 64mg; Fibre 1g; Sodium 79mg.

Madeleine cakes with raspberry buttercream

These madeleine-style cupcakes have a gorgeous pink crumb and little shell-shaped decorations made from the same mixture, pressed over a glamorous pink swirl of raspberry buttercream.

MAKES 9

115g/4oz/1 cup self-raising
   (self-rising) flour
100g/3½oz/scant ½ cup caster
   (superfine) sugar
3 eggs
115g/4oz/½ cup butter, melted
50g/2oz/½ cup ground almonds
5ml/1 tsp rose water

FOR THE TOPPING
75g/3oz/6 tbsp butter, softened
175g/6oz/1½ cups icing (confectioners')
   sugar, sifted
15ml/1 tbsp lemon juice
15ml/1 tbsp raspberry jam
few drops red food colouring

1 Preheat the oven to 190°C/375°F/ Gas 5. Line nine cups of a muffin tin (pan) with paper cases. Brush a mini madeleine mould with butter.

2 Sift the flour and salt into a bowl and stir in the sugar. Beat the eggs and mix into the sugar and flour, then add the cooled melted butter, ground almonds and rose water. Mix well. Cover and chill for 1 hour.

3 Fill the paper cases three-quarters full. Half-fill the mini madeleine mould with mixture. Bake for 5 minutes.

4 Bake the cakes for 20 minutes until risen and firm. Leave to cool then turn out on to a wire rack.

5 For the topping, beat the butter with the icing sugar until smooth. Stir in the lemon juice and jam and beat. Add a few drops of food colouring and beat until evenly coloured.

6 Fill a piping (pastry) bag fitted with a star nozzle with the buttercream. Pipe a whirl over the centre of each cake and press a madeleine lightly to one side of it.

Nutritional information per portion: Energy 364kcal/1523kJ; Protein 4.7g; Carbohydrate 39.3g, of which sugars 29.4g; Fat 22.1g, of which saturates 12g; Cholesterol 111mg; Calcium 58mg; Fibre 0.8g; Sodium 182mg.

Cupcakes with raspberry buttercream

This mouthwatering raspberry pink cream is great for party cakes, when it is piped into little rosettes. Top these cakes with a few fresh raspberries for an elegant finish.

MAKES 8–9

175g/6oz/3/4 cup butter, softened
175g/6oz/3/4 cup caster (superfine) sugar
5ml/1 tsp vanilla extract, or 5ml/
   1 tsp finely grated lemon rind
4 eggs, lightly beaten
175g/6oz/1½ cups self-raising (self-rising)
   flour, sifted

FOR THE TOPPING

175g/6oz/3/4 cup butter, softened
350g/12oz/3 cups icing (confectioners')
   sugar, sifted
25ml/1½ tbsp lemon juice
25ml/1½ tbsp raspberry jam
few drops red food colouring
fresh raspberries

1 Preheat the oven to 180°C/350°F/Gas 4. Line 8–9 cups of a bun tin (pan) with paper cases.

2 Beat the butter and sugar together until light and creamy. Add the vanilla or lemon rind.

3 Gradually add the eggs, beating well after each addition. Add the sifted flour and fold into the mixture until just combined.

4 Divide the mixture among the paper cases and bake for 20 minutes until the cakes are golden brown and the centres feel firm to the touch. Remove from the oven.

5 Leave to cool in the tin for 5 minutes, then turn out on to a wire rack to cool completely.

6 For the topping, beat the butter with the icing sugar until smooth and fluffy. Stir in the lemon juice and raspberry jam and continue to beat until smooth. Add the food colouring and beat until the buttercream is evenly coloured a pale pink.

7 Fill a piping (pastry) bag fitted with a star nozzle with the buttercream, and pipe small rosette shapes on to the cooled cakes. Decorate with fresh raspberries.

Nutritional information per portion: Energy 618kcal/2587kJ; Protein 5g; Carbohydrate 76.8g, of which sugars 62.4g; Fat 34.5g, of which saturates 21.7g; Cholesterol 174mg; Calcium 118mg; Fibre 0.6g; Sodium 396mg.

Double apricot and amaretto muffins

Amaretto has a special affinity with apricots (both fresh and dried ones are used here), and although it is an expensive addition, the scent alone makes it worthwhile.

MAKES 8–9

225g/8oz/1 cup plain (all-purpose) flour
12.5ml/2½ tsp baking powder
2.5ml/½ tsp ground cinnamon
115g/4oz/½ cup caster (superfine) sugar
75g/3oz/6 tbsp butter, melted
1 egg, beaten
150ml/¼ pint/⅔ cup buttermilk
**a handful ready-to-eat dried apricots,
    cut into strips**
2–3 amaretti, crumbled

FOR THE FRUIT AND GLAZE

**275g/10oz fresh apricots, stoned (pitted)
    cut into quarters**
15ml/1 tbsp apricot jam
15ml/1 tbsp clear honey
30ml/2 tbsp amaretto liqueur

1 Preheat the oven to 200°C/400°F/ Gas 6. Grease the cups of a muffin tin (pan) or line with paper cases.

2 First make the fruit glaze. Place the apricots on a baking tray. Add the apricot jam and honey. Bake for 5 minutes, basting once. Drizzle with amaretto. Leave to cool. Reduce oven temperature to 180°C/350°F/Gas 4.

3 Sift the dry muffin ingredients into a bowl. Mix the butter with the egg and buttermilk. Pour into the dry ingredients and part blend. Add the baked apricots, reserving the syrup.

4 Spoon the batter into the paper cases. Bake for 28 minutes, until well risen and firm to the touch.

5 Decorate the tops with the dried apricot strips and crumbled amaretti. Return to the oven for 4–5 minutes until the tops look golden. Leave to cool slightly.

6 Heat the reserved syrup in a small pan for 30 seconds, then brush the hot glaze on top of the muffins. When the cakes are cool enough to handle transfer them to a wire rack to go cold.

Nutritional information per portion: Energy 216kcal/909kJ; Protein 3.8g; Carbohydrate 34.5g, of which sugars 15g; Fat 7.9g, of which saturates 4.8g; Cholesterol 41mg; Calcium 68mg; Fibre 0.8g; Sodium 84mg.

Blackcurrant muffins with crimson frosting

Part-cooking the blackcurrants adds a pleasant tart-sweet flavour to the fruit. The syrupy juices left over from the cooked fruit are combined with icing sugar to make a luscious crimson frosting.

MAKES 9–10

75g/3oz/scant ¹/₂ cup caster (superfine) sugar
30ml/2 tbsp redcurrant jelly
25g/1oz/2 tbsp butter
225g/8oz/2 cups blackcurrants, topped and tailed, plus extra to decorate
225g/8oz/2 cups plain (all-purpose) flour
12.5ml/2¹/₂ tsp baking powder
150g/5oz/scant ³/₄ cup golden caster (superfine) sugar
75g/3oz/6 tbsp butter, melted
1 egg, lightly beaten
200ml/7fl oz/scant 1 cup buttermilk and milk mixed in equal quantities
5ml/1 tsp grated orange rind
icing (confectioners') sugar

1 Preheat the oven to 190°C/375°F/Gas 5. Line the cups of a muffin tin (pan) with paper cases.

2 Dissolve the caster sugar, redcurrant jelly and butter into a syrup, in a pan, over a low heat. Set aside a few blackcurrants for decoration. Put the rest in a baking tin (pan) and pour the syrup over. Bake for 8 minutes, stirring once. Set aside to cool. Turn the oven down to 180°C/350°F/Gas 4.

3 Sift the flour, baking powder and sugar into a bowl.

4 Make a well in the centre. Add the butter, egg, buttermilk mixture and orange rind. Fold in gently.

5 Blend the cooled fruit into the batter, reserving the syrup. Three-quarters fill the paper cases and bake for 22–25 minutes. Turn out on to a wire rack and leave to cool.

6 Mix the reserved syrup with enough icing sugar to make a soft frosting. Swirl the frosting over the cooled muffins. Add a few extra berries and serve immediately.

Nutritional information per portion: Energy 208kcal/875kJ; Protein 3.7g; Carbohydrate 29.9g, of which sugars 12.7g; Fat 9.1g, of which saturates 5.6g; Cholesterol 43mg; Calcium 78mg; Fibre 1.5g; Sodium 95mg.

Montebianco cupcakes

This recipe is based on a pudding called Marrons Mont Blanc in France and Montebianco in Italy: a sweetened chestnut purée is covered in thick vanilla cream. Anyone with a sweet tooth and a passion for chestnuts will find these little cakes especially delicious.

MAKES 10

75g/3oz/6 tbsp butter, softened
175g/6oz/¾ cup golden caster (superfine) sugar
115g/4oz/1 cup icing (confectioners') sugar
5ml/1 tsp vanilla extract
15ml/1 tbsp rum
4 eggs, separated
200g/7oz cooked and peeled whole
    chestnuts, ground

150g/5oz/1¼ cups plain (all-purpose) flour
10ml/2 tsp baking powder

FOR THE TOPPING
300ml/½ pint/1¼ cups double (heavy) cream
5ml/1 tsp vanilla extract
10ml/2 tsp caster (superfine) sugar
sifted cocoa powder, to dust

1 Preheat the oven to 180°C/350°F/Gas 4. Line the cups of a bun tin (pan) with paper cases.

2 Place the butter, caster sugar and icing sugar in a large bowl and beat until light and smooth using an electric mixer. Mix in the vanilla extract and rum.

3 Beat the egg yolks lightly and add them in a thin stream, beating well until the mixture is very smooth. Add the ground chestnuts and beat them in, then fold in the flour sifted together with the baking powder.

4 In a separate bowl beat the egg whites into fairly firm peaks and fold them lightly into the chestnut mixture until evenly combined.

5 Fill the cups three-quarters full with the cake mixture, and bake for 20–25 minutes, until the cakes are golden and the centres feel springy. Remove from the oven.

6 Leave the cakes in the tins for 5 minutes to cool, then turn them out on to a wire rack to cool.

7 To make the topping, beat the cream with the vanilla extract and caster sugar into soft peaks that hold their shape. Transfer to a large piping (pastry) bag fitted with a plain 5mm/¼in nozzle and pipe into tall piles on top of the cakes. To finish, dust the cream very lightly with sifted cocoa powder.

Nutritional information per portion: Energy 429kcal/1796kJ; Protein 5g; Carbohydrate 51.1g, of which sugars 33.8g; Fat 25.2g, of which saturates 13.8g; Cholesterol 132mg; Calcium 74mg; Fibre 1.3g; Sodium 100mg.

Carrot cupcakes

These wonderfully tasty cakes are made using an easy all-in-one recipe. The mixture is enriched with grated carrots, which add sweetness as well as keeping the cakes moist and light.

MAKES 8–10

225g/8oz/1 cup caster (superfine) sugar

3 eggs

200ml/7fl oz/scant 1 cup vegetable oil

grated rind and juice of 1 orange

225g/8oz/2 cups self-raising (self-rising)
    wholemeal (whole-wheat) flour

5ml/1 tsp ground cinnamon

2.5ml/½ tsp grated nutmeg

pinch of salt

350g/12oz grated carrot, squeezed dry

175g/6oz/1 cup walnuts, chopped

FOR THE TOPPING

225g/8oz/1 cup cream cheese

30ml/2 tbsp clear honey

15ml/1 tbsp orange juice

50g/2oz marzipan

orange food colouring

small quantity angelica

1 Preheat the oven to 180°C/350°F/ Gas 4. Line a bun tin (pan) with paper cases.

2 Beat the sugar, eggs, oil, orange rind and juice together until light and frothy. Sift in the flour, spices and salt and beat for a further minute. Stir in the carrots and nuts.

3 Fill the prepared paper cases and bake for 25 minutes, until the cakes are firm in the centre. Turn out on to a wire rack to cool.

4 For the icing, beat the cheese, honey and orange juice together. Chill for 30 minutes. Tint the marzipan orange with food colouring.

5 Break off small pieces and roll between your palms to form carrot shapes. Using a knife, press marks around the carrots and stick small pieces of angelica in the tops to resemble stalks.

6 Spread the icing over the tops of the cooled cakes. Arrange the carrots on the cakes.

Nutritional information per portion: Energy 542kcal/2258kJ; Protein 7.9g; Carbohydrate 46.9g, of which sugars 32.7g; Fat 37.1g, of which saturates 9.6g; Cholesterol 78mg; Calcium 75mg; Fibre 3.4g; Sodium 102mg.

Seville orange cupcakes

A few drops of Grand Marnier will add warmth to the flavour of this sharp-sweet butter frosting. Out of season, a sweet orange may be substituted for the Seville orange.

MAKES 8–9

175g/6oz/¾ cup butter, softened
175g/6oz/¾ cup caster (superfine) sugar
5ml/1 tsp finely grated lemon rind
4 eggs, lightly beaten
175g/6oz/1½ cups self-raising (self-rising) flour, sifted

FOR THE TOPPING

140g/5oz/10 tbsp butter, softened
250g/9oz/2¼ cups icing (confectioners') sugar
juice and finely grated rind of one Seville orange
5ml/1 tsp Grand Marnier
orange food colouring (optional)

1 Preheat the oven to 180°C/350°F/Gas 4. Line 8–9 cups of a bun tin (pan) with paper cases.

2 Place the butter and sugar in a mixing bowl. Beat together until light and creamy. Add the lemon rind. Gradually add the eggs, beating after each addition. Add the sifted flour and fold into the mixture with a large spoon until just combined.

3 Divide the mixture among the paper cases and bake for 20 minutes until the cakes are golden brown and the centres feel firm to the touch. Remove from the oven.

4 Leave to cool for 5 minutes, then turn the cakes out on to a wire rack to cool completely before decorating.

5 To make the topping, beat the softened butter until light and fluffy, using an electric mixer or a wooden spoon. Gradually add the sugar, orange juice and rind, Grand Marnier and a few drops of food colouring, if using, beating continuously until the mixture is smooth.

6 Cover the bowl and chill for several hours to allow the flavours to mature before using to top the cooled cakes.

Nutritional information per portion: Energy 659kcal/2749kJ; Protein 5g; Carbohydrate 64.5g, of which sugars 50.1g; Fat 44g, of which saturates 28g; Cholesterol 201mg; Calcium 114mg; Fibre 0.6g; Sodium 484mg.

Spangled sugar cupcakes

These cakes are made using a basic mixture, but are transformed by the original decoration using caramelized sugar spirals, which are not difficult to make.

MAKES 8–9

175g/6oz/³⁄4 cup butter, softened
175g/6oz/³⁄4 cup caster (superfine) sugar
5ml/1 tsp finely grated lemon rind
4 eggs, lightly beaten
175g/6oz/1¹⁄2 cups self-raising
   (self-rising) flour, sifted
115g/4oz cinder toffee (honeycomb), broken
   into small pieces

FOR THE PULLED SUGAR DECORATIONS
115g/4oz/¹⁄2 cup caster (superfine) sugar

1 Preheat the oven to 180°C/350°F/Gas 4. Line the cups of a bun tin (pan) with paper cake cases. Beat the butter with the sugar until light and creamy. Add the lemon rind. Gradually add the eggs in small amounts, beating after each addition.

2 Add the sifted flour and fold lightly into the mixture until just combined. Fold in the cinder toffee.

3 Spoon the mixture into the paper cases and bake for 20 minutes until the cakes are golden and firm. Allow to cool a little in the tin, then turn out on to a rack to cool completely.

4 To make the decorations, place the caster sugar in a non-stick pan over a high heat. Do not stir. When the sugar starts to turn into syrup around the edges tilt the pan to blend the sugar into the syrup. Continue until all the sugar has melted into a golden caramel. Remove the pan immediately from the heat and briefly sink its base in cold water. As the caramel cools it will become thicker; for sugar spirals it needs to be the consistency of golden (corn) syrup. If it thickens too much, gently warm it up.

5 To make the spirals, take one tablespoonful of the caramel and trail it over a greased sharpening steel, while turning the steel. Snap off the tail of the caramel and gently slide the spiral off. Leave on a lightly oiled tray while you make the remaining decorations. Gently press the sugar spirals at an angle on top of the cakes.

Nutritional information per portion: Energy 569kcal/2379kJ; Protein 5.6g; Carbohydrate 61.6g, of which sugars 46.7g; Fat 37.7g, of which saturates 21.7g; Cholesterol 173mg; Calcium 81mg; Fibre 0.6g; Sodium 203mg.

Pistachio and rose water cupcakes

Rose water and pistachios have a subtle affinity, and are used in this recipe to flavour a rich buttercream frosting. The green colour of the topping gives them an unusual appearance.

MAKES 8–9

175g/6oz/¾ cup butter, softened
175g/6oz/¾ cup caster (superfine) sugar
5ml/1 tsp vanilla extract
4 eggs, lightly beaten
175g/6oz/1½ cups self-raising
   (self-rising) flour, sifted

FOR THE TOPPING
115g/4oz/¾ cup pistachio nuts, shelled
140g/5oz/10 tbsp butter
115g/4oz/1 cup icing (confectioners')
   sugar, sifted
10ml/2 tsp milk
2–3 drops rose water, or to taste

1 Preheat the oven to 180°C/350°F/Gas 4. Line 8–9 cups of a bun tin (pan) with paper cases.

2 Beat together the butter and sugar until light and creamy. Add the vanilla. Gradually add the eggs, beating well after each addition. Add the sifted flour and fold it delicately into the mixture with a large spoon until just combined.

3 Divide the mixture among the paper cases and bake for 20 minutes until the cakes are golden and firm to the touch. Leave to cool for 5 minutes, then turn the cakes out on to a wire rack to cool completely before decorating.

4 For the topping, process the pistachio nuts in a blender until finely ground. Whisk the butter until soft and creamy. Whisking at a low speed, gradually beat in the sugar, pistachios and milk, alternating with the rose water, until smooth. Cover the cakes with the frosting and sprinkle over a few chopped pistachios.

Nutritional information per portion: Energy 566kcal/2357kJ; Protein 8.5g; Carbohydrate 47.5g, of which sugars 32.2g; Fat 39.4g, of which saturates 19.2g; Cholesterol 157mg; Calcium 84mg; Fibre 1.8g; Sodium 375mg.

Pistachio flower cupcakes

The pistachios add flavour and a delicate green colour to a basic friand cake mixture, which is lightly perfumed with rose water. These pretty cakes will delight any lover of Parisian-style cakes.

MAKES 12

175g/6oz/³⁄₄ cup butter, melted
5ml/1 tsp rose water
150g/5oz/1¹⁄₄ cups finely ground
   pistachios, sifted
225g/8oz/2 cups icing (confectioners')
   sugar, sifted, plus extra for dusting
70g/2¹⁄₂ oz/9 tbsp plain (all-purpose)
   flour, sifted
6 egg whites
2.5ml/¹⁄₂ tsp finely grated lemon rind
whole pistachio nuts, to decorate
   (optional)

1 Preheat the oven to 190°C/375°F/Gas 5. Grease 12 fluted bun tins (pans) with melted butter and dust lightly with flour.

2 Mix the melted butter and rose water in a small bowl, then set aside.

3 Put the ground pistachios in a large mixing bowl, reserving 25g/1oz for decorating the cakes. Stir in the sifted icing sugar and flour.

4 In a separate bowl, beat the egg whites lightly just to break them up. Add the egg whites to the dry ingredients and mix. Add the melted butter and lemon rind to the bowl and mix until just combined.

5 Pour the mixture into the prepared tins and bake for 16 minutes, until golden and springy. Leave to cool slightly then turn out on to a wire rack. Dust with the reserved ground pistachios. Half-cover them with a strip of paper and dust with icing sugar, then remove the paper and decorate with a few pistachio nuts.

Nutritional information per portion: Energy 282kcal/1177kJ; Protein 4.4g; Carbohydrate 25.2g, of which sugars 20.4g; Fat 18.9g, of which saturates 8.8g; Cholesterol 34mg; Calcium 35mg; Fibre 0.9g; Sodium 207mg.

Fish cakes

Multicoloured sugarpaste shapes make effective decorations with minimal effort. This technique makes good use of leftover scraps of different coloured sugarpastes, but the paste dries and hardens very quickly, so keep it well wrapped when you are not working with it.

MAKES 12

225g/8oz/1 cup butter, softened
225g/8oz/1 cup caster (superfine) sugar
4 eggs
225g/8oz/2 cups self-raising (self-rising) flour
115g/4oz/1 cup plain (all-purpose) flour
60ml/4 tbsp ground almonds
25ml/1½ tbsp lemon juice
15ml/1 tbsp milk

FOR THE MARBLED TOPPINGS
275g/10oz sugarpaste
paste food colouring in 5 colours
a little blue royal icing

FOR THE FISH DECORATIONS
150g/5oz sugarpaste
paste food colouring in 5 colours
1 egg white, lightly beaten

1 Preheat the oven to 180°C/350°F/Gas 4. Line a 12-cup bun tin (pan) with paper cases.

2 Beat the butter and sugar together until light and fluffy. Add two of the eggs, a little at a time, beating well after each addition. Beat in 15ml/1 tbsp of the flour. Gradually add the remaining eggs, then beat in another 15ml/1 tbsp flour.

3 Sift the remaining flours and fold in lightly with the almonds, lemon juice and milk. Fill the paper cases almost to the top. Bake for 25 minutes, until golden and springy. Transfer to a wire rack to go cold. Slice the top off each cake to level.

4 For the marbled toppings, divide the sugarpaste into five pieces and tint each piece a different colour. Divide each of the coloured pieces into 12 small balls. Dust the work surface with icing sugar. Press a ball of each colour together in a circle. Roll out and cut out a circle to fit the top of a cupcake using a scallop-edged cutter. Cut one for each cake.

5 For the fish, divide the sugarpaste into six pieces and tint each with a different food colour. Roll each piece into a sausage, 10cm/4in long and 1cm/½in thick. Paint each strip with egg white and sandwich together. Cut 12 slices from the slab. Roll out the slices and cut a fish shape out of each. Spread a little of the blue royal icing on to each cake. Press the marbled circles on to the cakes, and stick a fish on top.

Nutritional information per portion: Energy 504kcal/2121kJ; Protein 6.2g; Carbohydrate 79g, of which sugars 57.3g; Fat 20.4g, of which saturates 10.9g; Cholesterol 107mg; Calcium 94mg; Fibre 1.3g; Sodium 169mg.

Pear cakes with curled marzipan leaves

The glorious shapes and colours of fallen leaves inspired the decoration for these delicious cakes made with caramelized autumn fruit. If you prefer to make standard-sized cupcakes, cut the pears into chunks instead of halves.

MAKES 6–7 LARGE CAKES

3–4 small ripe pears
40g/1½ oz/3 tbsp butter
15ml/1 tbsp caster (superfine) sugar
45ml/3 tbsp water
225g/8oz/2 cups plain (all-purpose) flour
15ml/1 tbsp baking powder
10ml/2 tsp mixed (apple pie) spice
150g/5oz/¾ cup golden caster
    (superfine) sugar

1 egg, lightly beaten
5ml/1 tsp finely grated lemon rind
75g/3oz/6 tbsp butter, melted
300ml/½ pint/1¼ cups sour cream
20 pecan nuts, lightly crushed
50g/2oz marzipan
orange food colouring
sifted icing (confectioners') sugar

1 Preheat the oven to 180°C/350°F/Gas 4. Grease 6–7 10cm/4in-diameter muffin tins (pans) or line with mini panettone paper cases.

2 Peel and cut the pears into halves lengthways. Remove the cores but leave the short stems on the fruit if possible.

3 Place the butter, sugar and water in a small frying pan over a low to medium heat, then sauté the pear halves gently for 6 minutes until tender. Set aside to cool.

4 Sift the dry ingredients into a large bowl. In another bowl, stir the egg, lemon rind, warm melted butter and sour cream together, then gently fold into the dry ingredients, with the pecans, until blended.

5 Add a small amount of batter to each cup. Press one pear half into each, upright, then half-fill the tins with the remaining batter. Bake for 25 minutes. Leave to cool for 5 minutes, then turn out on to a rack.

6 Colour the marzipan, then roll out thinly. Cut out leaves with a cutter. Drape over a rolling pin to dry. Paint veins on the leaves with food colouring. Serve the cakes dusted with icing sugar and decorated with the leaves.

Nutritional information per portion: Energy 566kcal/2362kJ; Protein 7.1g; Carbohydrate 58.7g, of which sugars 33.9g; Fat 35.2g, of which saturates 15.5g; Cholesterol 91mg; Calcium 121mg; Fibre 3.2g; Sodium 155mg.

Chestnut and dark chocolate cupcakes

Chestnuts add an extra dimension to this rich chocolate icing, which is used as a topping for chocolatey sponge cakes. A real must for chocoholics!

MAKES 20

150g/5oz dark (bittersweet) chocolate
175ml/6fl oz/³⁄₄ cup single (light) cream
5ml/1 tsp vanilla extract
225g/8oz/1 cup golden caster
   (superfine) sugar
200g/7oz/scant 1 cup butter
3 eggs
225g/8oz/2 cups plain (all-purpose) flour
20g/³⁄₄ oz/2 tbsp unsweetened
   cocoa powder, and extra for dusting
10ml/2 tsp baking powder

FOR THE TOPPING
350g/12oz/1¹⁄₂ cup butter, softened
230g/8oz/2 cups icing (confectioners')
   sugar, sifted
350g/2oz can puréed chestnuts
239g/8oz dark (bittersweet)
   chocolate, melted

1 Preheat the oven to 190°C/375°F/Gas 5. Line the cups of two bun tins (pans) with paper cases. Melt the chocolate with the cream over a low heat, stirring constantly. Stir in the vanilla and set aside.

2 Beat the sugar and butter together until light and fluffy, then beat in the eggs one at a time. Sift the flour, cocoa powder and baking powder over the butter mixture and fold in, alternating with the chocolate cream, until the batter is combined.

3 Half-fill the prepared cups and lightly smooth the tops level. Bake for 20–25 minutes, until the centres are firm. Cool on a wire rack.

4 For the topping, whisk the butter until soft and creamy. Whisking at a low speed, gradually add the icing sugar and the chestnut purée in alternate spoonfuls. Continue to beat, adding the cooled melted chocolate, until thick and creamy. Spread the icing on to the cooled cakes. Dust with cocoa powder.

Nutritional information per portion: Energy 492kcal/2053kJ; Protein 3.9g; Carbohydrate 51.7g, of which sugars 36.8g; Fat 31.4g, of which saturates 19.6g; Cholesterol 98mg; Calcium 61mg; Fibre 1.2g; Sodium 236mg.

Beetroot and bitter chocolate muffins

Although it is not often used in baking, freshly cooked beetroot contrasts well with the rich, intense cocoa flavour of bitter chocolate.

MAKES 9–10

115g/4oz dark (bittersweet) chocolate
115g/4oz/½ cup butter
250g/9oz beetroot (beets), cooked
   and peeled
3 eggs, lightly beaten
225g/8oz/2 cups self-raising
   (self-rising) flour
2.5ml/½ tsp baking powder
200g/7oz/1 cup caster (superfine) sugar
20–30ml/1½–2 tbsp rye flour,
   for dusting

FOR THE FROSTING

250ml/8fl oz/1 cup double (heavy) cream
75g/3oz/⅓ cup soft light brown sugar
5ml/1 tsp vanilla extract
150g/5oz dark (bittersweet)
   chocolate, grated

1 Preheat the oven to 180°C/350°F/Gas 4. Lightly grease the cups of a muffin tin (pan) or line them with paper cases. Melt the chocolate and butter in a large heatproof bowl set over a pan of barely simmering water. Stir occasionally. Remove from the heat.

2 Grate the cooked beetroot using the medium blade of a cheese grater. Whisk the beetroot into the chocolate and butter mixture with the eggs. Sift the flour, baking powder and sugar into the mixture and fold in gently. Do not overmix. Spoon the batter into the prepared tin. Dust with the rye flour.

3 Bake for 25 minutes until risen and springy to the touch. Leave to cool for 5 minutes, then transfer to a wire rack to go completely cold.

4 For the frosting, put the cream, sugar and vanilla in a pan and heat until it reaches boiling point. Remove from the heat. Stir in the chocolate until melted. Cool. Spread over the tops of the cakes.

Nutritional information per portion: Energy 342kcal/1437kJ; Protein 5.4g; Carbohydrate 50g, of which sugars 30.2g; Fat 14.8g, of which saturates 8.7g; Cholesterol 85mg; Calcium 112mg; Fibre 1.5g; Sodium 218mg.

Coffee muffins with toffee fudge frosting

*With a dense texture and complex flavours these coffee muffins are truly a cake to savour.
The rich and sweet smooth toffee frosting is a contrast to the grainy textured cake.*

MAKES 10

100ml/3½ fl oz/scant ½ cup
   single (light) cream
10ml/2 tsp instant coffee granules
15ml/1 tbsp fine-ground roasted coffee
175g/6oz/¾ cup butter, softened
175g/6oz/¾ cup soft light brown sugar
2 eggs
100g/3¾ oz/scant 1 cup spelt flour
100g/3¾ oz/scant 1 cup self-raising
   (self-rising) flour

FOR THE FROSTING

75g/3oz/6 tbsp butter
75g/3oz/scant ½ cup light muscovado
   (brown) sugar
15ml/1 tbsp golden (light corn) syrup
5ml/1 tsp instant coffee granules
130g/4½ oz/generous 1 cup icing
   (confectioners') sugar, sifted
5ml/1 tsp lemon juice
candy-coated coffee beans, to decorate

1 Place the cream, instant and ground coffees in a small pan and bring to the boil. Remove from the heat. Set aside to cool. Preheat the oven to 180°C/350°F/Gas 4. Line the cups of a muffin tin (pan) with paper cases.

2 In a mixing bowl, beat the butter and sugar until light and creamy, then gradually beat in the eggs one at a time. Beat in the cooled coffee mixture until just combined. Sift the two flours into the creamed mixture and fold in until just combined. Do not overmix.

3 Three-quarters fill the paper cases with the batter. Bake for 20–25 minutes. Leave to stand for 5 minutes in the tin before turning out on to a wire rack to go completely cold.

4 To make the frosting, melt 50g/2oz/¼ cup of the butter with the sugar and golden syrup in a pan over a low heat, stirring occasionally. Dissolve the coffee in 50ml/2fl oz/¼ cup boiling water and add to the ingredients in the pan. Bring slowly to the boil, stirring frequently, then simmer for 3 minutes, stirring once or twice. Remove from the heat and pour into a large bowl.

5 Whisk in the icing sugar, then the lemon juice and remaining butter. Beat until smooth. Stand the bowl in iced water and stir until the mixture thickens. Spread on to the tops of the muffins. Decorate with candy-coated coffee beans.

Nutritional information per portion: Energy 441kcal/1846kJ; Protein 3.6g; Carbohydrate 56.7g, of which sugars 41.5g; Fat 23.8g, of which saturates 15.1g; Cholesterol 101mg; Calcium 56mg; Fibre 1.5g; Sodium 213mg.

Blueberry and chocolate cupcakes

Blueberries are one of the many fruits that combine deliciously with the richness of chocolate in cakes, while still retaining their own distinctive flavour.

MAKES 12

115g/4oz/½ cup butter
75g/3oz plain (semisweet)
    chocolate, chopped
200g/7oz/scant 1 cup sugar
1 egg, lightly beaten
250ml/8fl oz/1 cup buttermilk
10ml/2 tsp vanilla extract
275g/10oz/2½ cups plain
    (all-purpose) flour
5ml/1 tsp bicarbonate of soda
    (baking soda)
175g/6oz/generous 1 cup fresh or
    thawed frozen blueberries
25g/1oz plain (semisweet) chocolate,
    melted, to decorate

1 Preheat the oven to 190°C/375°F/Gas 5. Arrange 12 paper cases in a muffin tin (pan). Melt the butter and chocolate in a pan over a medium heat, stirring frequently, until smooth. Remove from the heat and allow to cool slightly.

2 Put the sugar in a mixing bowl, add the egg, buttermilk and vanilla extract, and pour in the chocolate mixture. Stir until smooth. Sift the flour and bicarbonate of soda over the mixture, then gently fold in until just blended. (The mixture should be slightly lumpy.)

3 Gently fold in the blueberries. Spoon the batter into the paper cases. Bake for 25–30 minutes, until a skewer inserted in the centre comes out with just a few crumbs attached. Remove from the oven and leave in the tin for 5 minutes, then turn the muffins out on to a wire rack to cool.

4 If serving warm, drizzle melted chocolate over the top of each, then serve. Otherwise, leave until cold before decorating.

Nutritional information per portion: Energy 203kcal/850kJ; Protein 3.9g; Carbohydrate 24.9g, of which sugars 6.6g; Fat 10.5g, of which saturates 6.4g; Cholesterol 39mg; Calcium 63mg; Fibre 1g; Sodium 90mg.

Chocolate and vanilla cupcakes

A snowy topping of thick, creamy mascarpone whipped with sugar and flecked with the fragrant black seeds of vanilla conceals a lovely dark chocolate cake.

MAKES 10

100g/3½oz/scant ½ cup caster (superfine) sugar
115g/4oz/1 cup self-raising (self-rising) flour, sifted
3 eggs, lightly beaten
115g/4oz/½ cup butter, melted
50g/2oz/½ cup ground almonds
5ml/1 tsp vanilla extract
50g/2oz dark (bittersweet) chocolate, melted

FOR THE TOPPING
½ vanilla pod (bean)
175g/6oz/¾ cup butter, softened
2.5ml/½ tsp finely grated lemon rind
350g/12oz/3 cups icing (confectioners') sugar, sifted, plus extra for dusting
225g/8oz/1 cup mascarpone

1 Preheat the oven to 180°C/350°F/Gas 4. Line a muffin tin (pan) with paper cases.

2 Mix the sugar with the flour. Stir in the eggs and add the melted butter, ground almonds and vanilla extract, followed by the melted chocolate. Stir together, then cover the bowl and chill for 30 minutes to 1 hour.

3 Spoon the mixture into the muffin cases, filling three-quarters full. Bake for 25 minutes, or until the cakes are firm. Leave to cool.

4 For the topping, scrape the seeds from the vanilla pod and reserve. Cut the pod into fine strips. In a bowl beat the butter, lemon rind, sugar and mascarpone until smooth. Stir in the vanilla seeds. Pipe on to the cakes. Dust with icing sugar and top with the vanilla strips.

Nutritional information per portion: Energy 608kcal/2537kJ; Protein 5.3g; Carbohydrate 59.6g, of which sugars 50.4g; Fat 40.4g, of which saturates 23.9g; Cholesterol 146mg; Calcium 89mg; Fibre 0.7g; Sodium 310mg.

Chocolate truffle muffins

Not an everyday muffin, these luscious chocolate treats with a hidden truffle centre and equally sinful soft chocolate frosting are decorated with pretty seashell chocolates. The chocolates can be bought or you could make your own using plastic moulds. Eat fresh.

MAKES 9 STANDARD MUFFINS

165g/5½ oz/scant ¾ cup butter, softened
150g/5oz/⅔ cup light muscovado (brown) sugar
3 eggs, lightly beaten
150g/5oz self-raising (self-rising) flour
25g/1oz/¼ cup unsweetened cocoa powder
7.5ml/1½ tsp baking powder

FOR THE TRUFFLES
150g/5oz dark (bittersweet) chocolate,
  broken into pieces

20ml/4 tsp double (heavy) cream
20ml/4 tsp brandy (optional)

FOR THE FROSTING
250ml/8fl oz/1 cup double (heavy) cream
75g/3oz/⅓ cup soft light brown sugar
5ml/1 tsp vanilla extract
150g/5oz dark (bittersweet) chocolate, grated

1 Preheat the oven to 180°C/350°F/Gas 4. Line the cups of a muffin tin (pan) with paper cases.

2 First make the truffles. Melt the chocolate in a heatproof bowl set over a pan of simmering water. Remove from the heat, and stir in the cream and the brandy (if using). Set aside to cool and thicken. Scoop the cool mixture into 9 balls.

3 To make the muffins, in a bowl, beat the butter and sugar. Beat in the eggs. Sift in the flour, cocoa and baking powder and mix lightly.

4 Half fill the paper cases. Add a truffle to the centre. Spoon the remaining cake batter on top. Bake for 22–25 minutes or until risen and springy to the touch. Cool.

5 For the frosting, put the cream, sugar and vanilla in a pan and heat until it reaches boiling point. Remove from the heat. Stir in the chocolate until melted. Cool.

6 Spread the frosting on top of each of the cold muffins and decorate with chocolate seashells.

Nutritional information per portion: Energy 331kcal/1381kJ; Protein 3.6g; Carbohydrate 28.6g, of which sugars 27.4g; Fat 23.5g, of which saturates 14.3g; Cholesterol 110mg; Calcium 32mg; Fibre 0.3g; Sodium 191mg.

Chocolate mint-filled cupcakes

These dark chocolate cakes have a sensational surprise inside: a luscious mint cream filling.
For even more mint flavour, try folding eight chopped mint chocolates into the cake batter.

MAKES 12

150g/5oz/⅔ cup unsalted (sweet)
   butter, softened
300g/11oz/1½ cups caster
   (superfine) sugar
3 eggs
250ml/8fl oz/1 cup milk
5ml/1 tsp peppermint extract
225g/8oz/2 cups plain (all-purpose) flour
pinch of salt
5ml/1 tsp bicarbonate of soda (baking soda)
50g/2oz/½ cup unsweetened
   cocoa powder

FOR THE FILLING AND TOPPING
300ml/10fl oz/1¼ cups whipping cream
10ml/2 tsp peppermint extract
175g/6oz plain (semisweet) chocolate
115g/4oz/½ cup butter

1 Preheat the oven to 180°C/350°F/Gas 4. Arrange 12 paper cases in a bun tin (pan).

2 Beat together the butter and sugar until creamy. Beat in the eggs, milk and peppermint. Sift the flour, salt, bicarbonate of soda and cocoa powder over the batter and mix in. Fill the cases with the batter. Bake for 15 minutes, until a skewer inserted into the centre comes out clean. Cool on a wire rack.

3 For the filling, whip the cream with 5ml/1tsp of the peppermint until it holds its shape. Pipe about 15ml/1 tbsp into the centre of each muffin.

4 To make the topping, in a pan over a low heat melt the chocolate and butter. Remove from the heat and stir in the remaining peppermint extract.

5 Leave to cool, then spread on to the top of each of the cupcakes.

Nutritional information per portion: Energy 555kcal/2315kJ; Protein 6.1g; Carbohydrate 52.3g, of which sugars 36.8g; Fat 38.6g, of which saturates 23.1g; Cholesterol 133mg; Calcium 98mg; Fibre 1.1g; Sodium 247mg.

Chocolate and sour cherry cakes

Sour cherries have an intense, tangy flavour, a contrast to the sweetness of white chocolate. These muffins are topped with a vibrantly fruity sour cherry and white chocolate icing.

MAKES 10

225g/8oz/2 cups plain (all-purpose) flour
10ml/2 tsp baking powder
pinch of salt
75g/3oz/⅓ cup golden caster
   (superfine) sugar
75g/3oz/6 tbsp butter
130g/4½ oz milk chocolate
1 small (US medium) egg, lightly beaten
90ml/6 tbsp milk
5ml/1 tsp vanilla extract
5ml/1 tsp pure chocolate extract

FOR THE TOPPING
100g/3½ oz vanilla white chocolate
50g/2oz/½ cup icing (confectioners')
   sugar, sifted
40g/1½ oz butter
40g/1½ oz dried sour cherries,
   roughly chopped

1 Preheat the oven to 180°C/350°F/Gas 4. Grease the cups of a large muffin tin (pan). Sift the flour, baking powder and salt into a large mixing bowl and mix in the sugar. Set aside.

2 Melt the butter in a small pan. Remove from the heat. Break half the chocolate into the melted butter and stir until melted. Grate the remaining chocolate and set aside.

3 Whisk together the egg, milk, vanilla and chocolate extracts. Stir into the dry ingredients with the melted chocolate butter and the grated chocolate. Fold lightly together. Divide the batter among the muffin cups, filling them three-quarters full. Bake for 25 minutes until golden. Turn on to a rack to cool.

4 For the icing, melt the white chocolate in a bowl set over a pan of simmering water. Stir in the icing sugar and the butter. Add 15ml/1 tbsp warm water and mix until smooth. Add the dried fruit. Coat the tops of the cooled muffins.

Nutritional information per portion: Energy 369kcal/1546kJ; Protein 5.1g; Carbohydrate 47.2g, of which sugars 29.7g; Fat 19.1g, of which saturates 11.7g; Cholesterol 55mg; Calcium 112mg; Fibre 0.7g; Sodium 142mg.

Truffle cupcakes with Indian spices

These rich chocolate cakes, which have a fairly dense crumb, are lightly fragranced with warming Indian spices and topped generously with a smooth, buttery chocolate truffle mixture.

MAKES 20

150g/5oz dark (bittersweet) chocolate, broken up
250ml/8fl oz/1 cup single (light) cream
5ml/1 tsp vanilla extract
2.5ml/½ tsp ground cinnamon
5ml/1 tsp ground cardamom
225g/8oz/1 cup caster (superfine) sugar
200g/7oz/scant 1 cup butter
3 eggs, separated
225/8oz/2 cups plain (all-purpose) flour

20g/¾ oz/3 tbsp unsweetened cocoa powder,
    plus extra for dusting
10ml/2 tsp baking powder

FOR THE DECORATION

150ml/¼ pint/⅔ cup double (heavy) cream
350g/12oz dark chocolate
50g/2oz/4 tbsp butter
chocolate truffles

1 Preheat the oven to 180°C/350°F/Gas 4. Line the cups of two large bun tins (pans) with paper cases.

2 Put the chocolate and cream in a bowl set over a pan of simmering water. Stir continuously until the chocolate has melted and the mixture is smooth. Stir in the vanilla and spices and set aside.

3 Beat the sugar and butter together until light and fluffy, then gradually beat in the egg yolks one at a time. Put the egg whites in a dry, clean bowl and whisk them until they form stiff peaks. Set aside.

4 Sift the flour, cocoa powder and baking powder together and fold into the butter and sugar mixture, alternately with the spiced chocolate cream, until evenly combined. Do not overmix. Fold the egg whites lightly into the mixture. Spoon into the prepared cases and smooth the tops level. Bake for 20 minutes until the cakes are firm to the touch. Leave them in the tins for 5 minutes then turn out on to a wire rack to cool completely.

5 To make the topping, bring the cream to the boil, remove from the heat and leave for 1 minute. Break the chocolate into the cream, stir until smooth. Add the butter and continue to stir until glossy. Use immediately to top the cakes. Press cocoa-dusted truffles on to the top of each cake, and dust with a little extra sifted cocoa powder. Serve the cakes on the day of making.

Nutritional information per portion: Energy 380kcal/1587kJ; Protein 4g; Carbohydrate 37.6g, of which sugars 27.5g; Fat 25.2g, of which saturates 15.2g; Cholesterol 76mg; Calcium 54mg; Fibre 0.5g; Sodium 131mg.

Special occasions

Pretty cupcakes or muffins always look

lovely on a party table. A tiered cakestand

holding small cakes is a charming and popular

substitute for a traditional wedding cake,

but there is a design here for every occasion,

from iced cakes encrusted with brightly

coloured candies for a children's birthday

tea to sophisticated liqueur-laced creations

for grown-up feasts. Everyone will enjoy

helping themselves to their own beautifully

decorated little cake.

Kids' chocolate party muffins

A generous covering of bright and colourful sweets, sprinkles and marshmallows over a thick chocolate frosting is bound to go down well with children of all ages.

MAKES 9–10

165g/5½ oz/scant ¾ cup butter, softened
150g/5oz/¾ cup caster (superfine) sugar
5ml/1 tsp vanilla extract
150g/5oz/1¼ cups self-raising (self-rising) flour
20g/¾oz/scant ¼ cup unsweetened cocoa powder
7.5ml/1½ tsp baking powder
3 eggs, beaten
50–60 small sweets (candies)
coloured sprinkles

FOR THE FROSTING

250ml/8fl oz/1 cup crème fraîche
225g/8oz plain (semisweet) chocolate, broken into pieces
75g/3oz/¾ cup icing (confectioners') sugar

1 Preheat the oven to 180°C/350°F/Gas 4. Lightly grease the cups of a muffin tin (pan) or line them with paper cases.

2 In a large bowl, beat together the butter, sugar and vanilla until the mixture is light and creamy. Sift the flour, cocoa and baking powder into the butter and sugar mixture and beat to combine. Add the eggs and beat well.

3 Divide the batter between the paper cases and bake for 22–25 minutes or until risen and springy to the touch. Leave to stand for a few minutes then turn out on to a wire rack to go cold.

4 To make the frosting, heat the crème fraîche over a low heat until hot, but not boiling. Remove from the heat.

5 Add the chocolate and stir until melted. Sift in the icing sugar and mix until smooth. Set aside to thicken slightly. Spread in swirls over the muffins. Decorate with confectionery.

Nutritional information per portion: Energy 392kcal/1641kJ; Protein 5g; Carbohydrate 42.2g, of which sugars 30.5g; Fat 23.8g, of which saturates 14.8g; Cholesterol 111mg; Calcium 110mg; Fibre 0.7g; Sodium 235mg.

Marzipan-topped Easter cakes

These Easter cupcakes are irresistibly flavoured with fresh spices and orange zest and decorated with an embossed marzipan topping and cute little Easter motifs.

MAKES 10–11

115g/4oz dried mixed fruit, finely chopped
115g/4oz sultanas (golden raisins)
50g/2oz mixed (candied) peel, chopped
100ml/3½fl oz/scant ½ cup sherry
115g/4oz/½ cup butter, softened
115g/4oz/½ cup light muscovado
   (brown) sugar
2 eggs
225g/8oz/2 cups self-raising (self-rising)
   flour
7.5ml/1½ tsp mixed (apple pie) spice
finely grated rind of ½ large orange and
   juice of ¼ orange

FOR THE GLAZE AND TOPPING
30ml/2 tbsp apricot jam
15ml/1 tbsp water
15ml/1 tbsp caster (superfine) sugar
450g/1lb marzipan
small amounts of coloured sugarpaste
sugared eggs

1 Place the dried mixed fruit, sultanas and mixed peel in a bowl. Add the sherry and stir well. Leave for 24 hours.

2 Preheat the oven to 180°C/350°F/Gas 4. Line the cups of a bun tin (pan) with paper cases.

3 Beat the butter and sugar until creamy. Beat in an egg. Add 15ml/1 tbsp of flour and mix well before repeating with the second egg and another 15ml/ 1 tbsp flour. Fold in the remaining flour and mixed spice. Drain the dried fruit and stir it in with the orange rind and juice.

4 Fill the paper cases three-quarters full. Bake for 25 minutes until springy to the touch. Allow to cool. Slice off the tops level with the top of the cases.

5 Put the apricot jam, water and sugar in a pan and melt over a low heat. Roll out the marzipan to 3mm/⅛in thick. Emboss with circular patterns. Cut out round shapes and attach to the cakes using the jam mixture. Cut out a selection of motifs from sugarpaste, dry, then stick on with a few sugared eggs.

Nutritional information per portion: Energy 452kcal/1903kJ; Protein 5.8g; Carbohydrate 73.7g, of which sugars 58.1g; Fat 15.1g, of which saturates 6.5g; Cholesterol 59mg; Calcium 85mg; Fibre 2g; Sodium 127mg.

You're a star!

Mascarpone and Marsala add a delicious nuance to these mocha-flavoured cakes, which are topped with a smooth velvety cream and decorated with chocolate stars. You can make the chocolate decorations in advance and keep them in an airtight box in the refrigerator.

MAKES 8–10

150g/5oz/10 tbsp butter, softened
200g/7oz/scant 1 cup golden caster
   (superfine) sugar
3 eggs
175g/6oz/³⁄₄ cup mascarpone
5ml/1 tsp grated lemon rind
30ml/2 tbsp buttermilk
15ml/1 tbsp unsweetened cocoa powder, plus
   extra for dusting
25ml/1¹⁄₂ tbsp espresso coffee
15ml/1 tbsp Marsala
250g/9oz/2¹⁄₄ cups self-raising (self-rising) flour

FOR THE TOPPING AND DECORATION

250ml/8fl oz/1 cup double (heavy) cream
225g/8oz/1 cup mascarpone
15ml/1 tbsp golden caster (superfine) sugar
15ml/1 tbsp Marsala
seeds from ¹⁄₂ vanilla pod (bean)
25g/1oz milk chocolate, melted
100g/3¹⁄₂ oz plain (semisweet) chocolate
100g/3¹⁄₂ oz milk chocolate

1 Preheat the oven to 180°C/350°F/Gas 4. Line a muffin tin (pan) with paper cases.

2 Beat the butter and sugar together until light and creamy. Gradually beat in the eggs, one at a time, beating well after each addition. Stir in the mascarpone, lemon rind, buttermilk, cocoa, coffee and Marsala, then fold in the flour.

3 Fill the prepared cups. Bake for 25 minutes, or until firm to the touch. Turn out on to a wire rack to cool.

4 Meanwhile, make the topping. Beat the cream with the mascarpone, sugar, Marsala and vanilla seeds. Lightly fold in the melted chocolate.

5 To make the decorations, melt the chocolates separately, then spread on baking parchment and chill until just set. Cut out the shapes. Spoon the topping on to the cakes, and press on the decorations. Dust with cocoa powder.

Nutritional information per portion: Energy 718kcal/2990kJ; Protein 8g; Carbohydrate 56.8g, of which sugars 36.7g; Fat 53.7g, of which saturates 32.1g; Cholesterol 167mg; Calcium 146mg; Fibre 1g; Sodium 297mg.

Lovebirds

Unashamedly romantic decorations make these cakes perfect for any occasion when love is in the air, from an intimate tryst to an engagement or anniversary party.

MAKES 10

175g/6oz/¾ cup butter, softened
175g/6oz/¾ cup caster (superfine) sugar
4 eggs, lightly beaten
5ml/1 tsp vanilla extract
175g/6oz/1½ cups self-raising
  (self-rising) flour, sifted

FOR THE ICING AND DECORATIONS

350g/12oz/3 cups icing (confectioners')
  sugar, sifted
115g/4oz white sugarpaste
food colour in different tints

1 Preheat the oven to 180°C/350°F/Gas 4. Line a bun tin (pan) with paper cases.

2 Beat the butter with the sugar until creamy. Beat in the eggs one at a time, then stir in the vanilla and flour.

3 Half-fill the paper cases with the batter. Bake for 20 minutes, until golden. Cool on a wire rack.

4 Tint the sugarpaste and cut out scalloped circles to fit the cake tops.

5 Make the glacé icing, then tint it and spread a little on each cake. Stick one scallop to each cake top.

6 Cut out lovebirds, hearts, flowers, and leaves from sugarpaste and leave to dry. Stick them in place with sugarpaste and icing.

Nutritional information per portion: Energy 385kcal/1614kJ; Protein 4.9g; Carbohydrate 52.8g, of which sugars 38g; Fat 18.6g, of which saturates 11.2g; Cholesterol 129mg; Calcium 62mg; Fibre 0.6g; Sodium 180mg.

Mini party cakes

Once these pretty party cakes are iced, a sherbet 'flying saucer' sweet is stuck on top of each one, before being decorated with butterflies and flowers.

MAKES 48 TINY CAKES

175g/6oz/³⁄4 cup butter, softened
175g/6oz/³⁄4 cup caster (superfine) sugar
4 eggs, lightly beaten
5ml/1 tsp vanilla extract
175g/6oz/1¹⁄2 cups self-raising (self-rising) flour, sifted

FOR THE ICING AND DECORATIONS
150g/5oz/1¹⁄4 cups icing (confectioners') sugar, sifted
food colouring in 4 colours
115g/4oz white sugarpaste
sherbet-filled flying saucer sweets (candies)

1 Preheat the oven to 180°C/350°F/ Gas 4. Line the cups of four 12-cup mini cupcake trays with paper cases.

2 Beat the butter and sugar until light and creamy. Gradually add the eggs and beat well after each addition. Add the vanilla and flour and fold into the butter mixture until just combined.

3 Half-fill the paper cases and bake for 12 minutes until golden. Leave on a wire rack to cool completely.

4 Make the icing with just enough hot water (about 20ml/4 tsp) to make a soft glacé icing. Divide the icing between four bowls, then tint each with a different food colour, keeping the colours pale.

5 Ice each cake. Decorate flying saucer sweets with tinted sprinkles and sugarpaste flowers, leaves and butterflies. Attach with glacé icing. Stick each to the top of a cupcake with glacé icing.

Nutritional information per portion: Energy 78kcal/329kJ; Protein 0.9g; Carbohydrate 11.6g, of which sugars 8.9g; Fat 3.5g, of which saturates 2.1g; Cholesterol 24mg; Calcium 20mg; Fibre 0.1g; Sodium 47mg.

Spice muffins with dove-shaped cookies

This muffin recipe has three personalities. Warm from the oven and spread with butter it makes a light breakfast treat; decorated with a cookie it makes a filling cake for teatime; add the simple frosting and you have a luxurious creation for a special occasion. Eat fresh.

MAKES 5 JUMBO MUFFINS

90g/3½oz/½ cup golden caster
   (superfine) sugar
200g/7oz/scant 1 cup clear honey
grated rind of 1 large orange
150g/5oz/1¼ cups rye flour
175g/6oz/1½ cups plain (all-purpose) flour
10ml/2 tsp baking powder
pinch of mixed (apple pie) spice
pinch of ground cloves
pinch of ground cinnamon
1 egg yolk

FOR THE DOVE COOKIES

50g/2oz/¼ cup soft light brown sugar
50g/2oz/4 tbsp butter, softened
90g/3½oz/scant 1 cup plain (all-purpose) flour
5ml/1 tsp baking powder
2.5ml/½ tsp ground cinnamon
2.5ml/½ tsp ground ginger
2.5ml/½ tsp freshly grated nutmeg
12.5ml/2½ tsp milk, or buttermilk
silver balls for eyes

FOR THE FROSTING

1 egg white
icing (confectioners') sugar, sifted

1 Preheat the oven to 180°C/350°F/Gas 4. Line the cups of a jumbo muffin tin (pan) with paper cases.

2 For the muffins, put 120ml/4fl oz/¼ cup water, the sugar, honey and orange rind in a pan and heat gently until the sugar dissolves, stirring occasionally. Leave to cool slightly.

3 Sift the flours, baking powder and spices into a large bowl. Make a well in the centre. Add half the honey liquid with the egg yolk and stir lightly. Add the remaining honey liquid and stir until just combined.

4 Spoon the batter into the paper cases. Bake for 30–35 minutes until risen and golden, then leave to stand for a few minutes. Transfer to a wire rack to cool completely. Turn the oven to 150°C/300°F/Gas 2. Lightly grease a baking sheet.

5 To make the cookies, in a bowl, beat the sugar and butter together. Sift in the dry ingredients and mix to combine, adding milk as you work. Knead the dough lightly with your hands until it is smooth. On a lightly floured surface, roll the dough to a 5mm/¼in thickness and cut out dove shapes, using a template if you like.

6 Place on the baking sheet and bake for 17–18 minutes. Leave to set for a few minutes on the sheet, then carefully transfer to a wire rack to go completely cold.

7 Mix the frosting ingredients together and spread most over the tops of the muffins, reserving a little of the frosting to decorate the cookies. Fill a piping bag fitted with a plain nozzle with the reserved frosting. Pipe your choice of decoration. Add a silver ball for an eye.

Nutritional information per portion: Energy 601kcal/2549kJ; Protein 8.8g; Carbohydrate 124.8g, of which sugars 60.6g; Fat 10.9g, of which saturates 6g; Cholesterol 63mg; Calcium 112mg; Fibre 5.2g; Sodium 86mg.

Christening cupcakes

Everyone will love these delicate little cakes, which are perfect for a christening party. Adorn the tops with cute decorations – rabbits, rocking horses and tiny spring flowers.

MAKES 48 TINY CAKES

175g/6oz/¾ cup butter, softened
175g/6oz/¾ cup caster (superfine) sugar
4 eggs, lightly beaten
5ml/1 tsp vanilla extract
175g/6oz/1½ cups self-raising
  (self-rising) flour, sifted

FOR THE CLEMENTINE ICING

150g/5oz/1¼ cups icing (confectioners')
  sugar, sifted
freshly squeezed juice of 1 clementine
  or mandarin

FOR THE DECORATIONS

115g/4oz sugarpaste divided and half
  tinted pink and half blue

1 Preheat the oven to 180°C/350°F/Gas 4. Line the cups of four 12-cup mini cupcake trays with paper cases.

2 Beat the butter and sugar until light and creamy. Add the beaten eggs in small amounts and beat well after each addition. Stir in the vanilla extract. Add the sifted flour and fold it into the mixture using a metal spoon, until just combined.

3 Half-fill the paper cases with the cake mixture. Bake for 12–15 minutes until golden. Test by lightly pressing the centre of the cakes with your finger: the sponge should lightly spring back. Leave on a wire rack to cool.

4 For the icing, stir the clementine juice into the icing sugar until smooth and shiny. Spread a little icing over the top of each cake, coaxing it lightly with a knife to coat the surface evenly.

5 Cut out sugarpaste decorations and arrange before the icing sets.

Nutritional information per portion: Energy 78kcal/329kJ; Protein 0.9g; Carbohydrate 11.6g, of which sugars 8.9g; Fat 3.5g, of which saturates 2.1g; Cholesterol 24mg; Calcium 20mg; Fibre 0.1g; Sodium 47mg.

Valentine cupcakes

Pink and white sugared hearts make a classic cake decoration that's very easy to achieve, using a few cutters in different sizes. Mix and match the colours and designs for a contemporary twist.

MAKES 10

175g/6oz/³⁄4 cup butter, softened
175g/6oz/³⁄4 cup caster (superfine) sugar
4 eggs, lightly beaten
5ml/1 tsp vanilla extract
175g/6oz/1¹⁄2 cups self-raising
    (self-rising) flour, sifted

FOR THE TOPPING

350g/12oz icing (confectioners') sugar,
    sifted
115g/4oz white sugarpaste
pink food colouring
pink candy sugar or sprinkles

1 Preheat the oven to 180°C/350°F/Gas 4. Line the cups of a bun tin (pan) with paper cases.

2 Beat the butter and sugar until light and creamy. Gradually add the beaten eggs and beat well after each addition. Stir in the vanilla extract. Add the sifted flour and fold it into the mixture until just combined.

3 Spoon the mixture into the paper cases. Bake for 20 minutes until golden. Test by lightly pressing the centre of the cakes with your finger: the sponge should lightly spring back. Leave on a wire rack to cool completely.

4 For the topping, mix the sugar with enough hot water to make a thick icing. Divide between two bowls and tint one pink. Spread on to the cakes.

5 Cut out heart shapes in different shades of pink sugarpaste. Paint some with water and cover with candy sugar or sprinkles. When dry, stick on to the cakes.

Nutritional information per portion: Energy 501kcal/2109kJ; Protein 5g; Carbohydrate 83.6g, of which sugars 68.8g; Fat 18.6g, of which saturates 11.2g; Cholesterol 129mg; Calcium 78mg; Fibre 0.6g; Sodium 181mg.

Fairy cupcakes

This easy recipe uses a basic mixture. The cakes are decorated with a buttercream topping. The delicate pearlized effect is achieved using edible lustre powder, available from sugarcraft suppliers. Add a tiny silver fairy decoration to complete the magical effect.

MAKES 8–9

175g/6oz/3/4 cup butter, softened
175g/6oz/3/4 cup caster (superfine) sugar
5ml/1 tsp vanilla extract
4 eggs, lightly beaten
175g/6oz/1 1/2 cups self-raising (self-rising) flour
silver dragées, fairy, and edible lustre powder,
    to decorate

FOR THE BUTTERCREAM

75g/3oz/6 tbsp butter, softened
175g/6oz/1 1/2 cups icing (confectioners') sugar,
    double sifted, plus extra for dusting
1/2 vanilla pod (bean), split

1 Preheat the oven to 180°C/350°F/Gas 4. Line the cups of a bun tin (pan) with paper cases.

2 Place the butter and sugar in a large bowl, and beat until light and creamy using an electric mixer. Add the vanilla extract and beat in the eggs in small amounts, beating well after each addition.

3 Sift the flour over and fold it gently into the mixture.

4 Spoon the mixture into the cases and bake for 20 minutes until the cakes are golden brown and the centres feel firm when pressed.

5 Leave the cakes in the tin for 5 minutes to cool, then transfer to a wire rack to cool completely.

6 To make the buttercream, beat the butter with the sugar and vanilla seeds until smooth and fluffy.

7 Spoon a thick blob of buttercream on to the top of each cake and smooth it over the surface, but not right up to the edges. Brush the tops of the cakes with edible lustre powder and top each one with silver dragées. Decorate with a silver fairy.

Nutritional information per portion: Energy 457kcal/1914kJ; Protein 4.9g; Carbohydrate 55.7g, of which sugars 40.9g; Fat 25.4g, of which saturates 15.7g; Cholesterol 148mg; Calcium 65mg; Fibre 0.6g; Sodium 242mg.

Mother's Day fairy cakes with sugar roses

These deliciously featherlight sponge cakes are topped with delicately coloured icing scented with rose water and trimmed with a feminine melange of sugarpaste flower decorations.

MAKES 10

3 eggs, separated
115g/4oz/½ cup caster (superfine) sugar
juice of ½ lemon
grated rind of 1 mandarin
65g/2½ oz/scant ½ cup fine semolina
15g/½ oz/1 tbsp ground almonds

FOR THE ROSE WATER ICING

350g/12oz/3 cups icing
   (confectioners') sugar
5ml/1 tsp rose water
15ml/1 tbsp hot water

FOR THE DECORATIONS

350g/12oz white sugarpaste
food colouring

1 Preheat the oven to 180°C/350°F/Gas 4. Line the cups of a bun tin (pan) with foil or paper cases.

2 Beat the egg yolks with the sugar until light. Beat in the lemon juice and fold in the mandarin rind, semolina and almonds. In a separate bowl, whisk the egg whites until stiff. Fold into the mixture.

3 Pour into the cake cases until half full. Bake for 15 minutes, until the cakes are golden. Leave to cool, then turn out on to a wire rack to cool completely.

4 To make the icing, mix the sugar with the rose water and enough hot water to make a flowing consistency. Spread on top of the cooled cakes and leave to dry.

5 To make the sugarpaste roses, tint some paste pink and roll out 3–4 small circles very thinly; roll up the first to form the centre, then add the other petals, working around the central petal. Keep the petals open at the top so that they start to resemble an unfurling bud. Set all the flowers on a board covered with baking parchment to dry. Stick in place with a blob of icing.

Nutritional information per portion: Energy 306kcal/1302kJ; Protein 3.2g; Carbohydrate 72g, of which sugars 66.9g; Fat 2.6g, of which saturates 0.5g; Cholesterol 57mg; Calcium 47mg; Fibre 0.3g; Sodium 26mg.

Summer cupcakes with fresh fruit icing

Add a touch of indulgence to a summer tea party with these gloriously pretty cupcakes. The recipe is simple and the cakes are topped with a trio of icings flavoured with fresh fruit juice.

MAKES 12

225g/8oz/1 cup butter, softened
225g/8oz/1 cup caster (superfine) sugar
4 eggs, lightly beaten
50g/2oz/½ cup plain (all-purpose) flour
150g/5oz/1¼ cups ground almonds
5ml/1 tsp vanilla extract
15ml/1 tbsp single (light) cream

FOR THE DECORATIONS
350g/12oz white sugarpaste
food colouring
royal icing
artificial flower stamens
candy sugar, for sprinkling
350g/12oz/3 cups icing (confectioners')
   sugar, sifted
15ml/1 tbsp fresh raspberry juice
15ml/1 tbsp fresh orange juice
15ml/1 tbsp fresh lime juice

1 Preheat the oven to 180°C/350°F/Gas 4. Line the cups of a bun tin (pan) with paper cases. Beat the butter and sugar until light and creamy.

2 Add the eggs in small amounts, beating after each addition. Sift in the flour and beat well. Add the ground almonds, vanilla extract and cream and combine. Part fill the paper cases and bake for 20 minutes until golden brown and firm. Cool in the tin for 5 minutes, then turn on to a wire rack to cool completely.

3 To make the flowers, tint pieces of paste as desired. Roll out and stamp out individual petals. Stick together in a flower shape. Mount some stamens in royal icing. Leave to dry. Cut out small flowers using plunger cutters. When the decorations are dry, make the icing for the cake tops. Divide the sugar among three bowls and mix each batch with one of the fruit juices and about 5ml/1 tsp hot water to make a smooth fluid icing.

4 Spread each icing on top of the cakes. Arrange the decorations on the cakes before the icing sets. Once it is dry, sprinkle over a little candy sugar.

Nutritional information per portion: Energy 536kcal/2253kJ; Protein 5.6g; Carbohydrate 78.4g, of which sugars 74.9g; Fat 24.4g, of which saturates 11.4g; Cholesterol 107mg; Calcium 87mg; Fibre 1.1g; Sodium 171mg.

Party number cakes

These delicious, moist Madeira cakes have a hidden centre of tangy lemon curd. The pretty pastel-coloured alphabet candies that decorate them can be arranged to spell out the names of your guests, if you wish. Look out for delicately coloured sweets and sprinkles to complete the effect.

MAKES 12

225g/8oz/1 cup butter, softened
225g/8oz/1 cup caster (superfine) sugar
4 eggs
225g/8oz/2 cups self-raising (self-rising) flour
115g/4oz/1 cup plain (all-purpose) flour
60ml/4 tbsp ground almonds
25ml/1½ tbsp lemon juice
15ml/1 tbsp milk
60ml/4 tbsp lemon curd

FOR THE SHERBET ICING

250g/9oz/2¼ cups icing (confectioners') sugar,
    double sifted
40g/1½ oz/⅓ cup sherbet
30ml/2 tbsp lemon juice
20ml/4 tsp hot water
15ml/1 tbsp lemon curd

FOR THE DECORATIONS

60 alphabet sweets (candies)
36 torpedo sweets (candies)
candy sugar or sprinkles

1 Preheat the oven to 180°C/350°F/Gas 4. Line the cups of a 12-cup muffin tin (pan) with paper cases.

2 Cream the butter and sugar until light and fluffy. Beat in two eggs a little at a time, then 15ml/1 tbsp of the flour. Add the remaining eggs, and another 15ml/1 tbsp of flour. Sift the remaining flours in, then fold them in lightly with the ground almonds, lemon juice and milk.

3 Fill the paper cups almost to the top. Bake for 20–25 minutes until the cakes are golden. Allow to cool.

4 To make the sherbet icing, sift the sugar and sherbet and combine with the remaining ingredients to make a soft icing that is just firm enough to hold its shape.

5 When the cakes are cold, slice a round from the top of each one. Insert 5ml/1 tsp lemon curd into each cake before replacing the top. Spread each cake with a layer of sherbet icing. Press your decorations into the icing while it is soft.

Nutritional information per portion: Energy 464kcal/1950kJ; Protein 6.2g; Carbohydrate 67.7g, of which sugars 44.6g; Fat 20.7g, of which saturates 11g; Cholesterol 108mg; Calcium 87mg; Fibre 1.3g; Sodium 173mg.

Iced cherry cakes

Glacé cherries are used in this almond cake mixture, but you could use sharp-tasting dried sour cherries, or even fresh cherries. A textured rolling pin is used for the embossed basketweave icing.

MAKES 10

175g/6oz/1½ cups self-raising
   (self-rising) flour
10ml/2 tsp baking powder
75g/3oz/¾ cup ground almonds
175g/6oz/¾ cup butter, softened
175g/6oz/¾ cup golden caster
   (superfine) sugar
3 eggs, lightly beaten
finely grated rind of ½ lemon
finely grated rind of ½ orange
15ml/1 tbsp brandy or Calvados
60ml/4 tbsp orange juice
150g/5oz glacé (candied) cherries, halved

FOR THE TOPPING
350g/12oz sugarpaste
green food colouring

FOR THE DECORATIONS
150g/5oz sugarpaste
red and brown food colouring
115g/4oz royal icing

1 Preheat the oven to 180°C/350°F/Gas 4. Line the cups of a bun tin (pan) with paper cases.

2 Sift the flour and baking powder into a large mixing bowl and stir in the ground almonds.

3 In another bowl beat the butter and sugar until creamy. Add one egg at a time and beat until the mixture is light and fluffy. Mix in the fruit rind, brandy and orange juice, then the dry ingredients and the cherries.

4 Fill the paper cases three-quarters full. Bake for 25 minutes or until golden and springy to the touch. Leave to cool a little before turning them out on to a wire rack.

5 For the topping, colour the sugarpaste pale green and roll it out to a 6mm/¼in thickness. Emboss with a decorative rolling pin, then cut out 10 circles and stick them on the cooled cakes using royal icing. Roll 20 red sugarpaste cherries, 20 brown stems and some green leaves and stick in place.

Nutritional information per portion: Energy 548kcal/2308kJ; Protein 5.6g; Carbohydrate 90.4g, of which sugars 76.9g; Fat 20.4g, of which saturates 10.3g; Cholesterol 97mg; Calcium 96mg; Fibre 1.2g; Sodium 162mg.

Wedding anniversary cakes

Featherlight cakes and simple white and mauve sugarpaste hearts make an elegant presentation for an anniversary celebration. Use heart-shaped and flower-shaped cutters for the decorations.

MAKES 10

3 eggs, separated
115g/4oz/$\frac{1}{2}$ cup caster (superfine) sugar
juice of $\frac{1}{2}$ lemon
grated rind of 1 mandarin
65g/2$\frac{1}{2}$ oz/scant $\frac{1}{2}$ cup fine semolina
15g/$\frac{1}{2}$oz/1 tbsp ground almonds

FOR THE ICING

350g/12oz/3 cups icing
   (confectioners') sugar
5ml/1 tsp grappa
15ml/1 tbsp hot water

FOR THE DECORATIONS

350g/12oz white sugarpaste
mauve food colouring
a little royal icing

1 To make the decorations, divide the sugarpaste in half. Knead a little mauve food colouring into one piece until evenly coloured, then roll out both pieces separately. Cut out 10 mauve hearts and 10 white hearts. Cut out 20 small flowers and pipe a little royal icing into each centre. Leave to dry.

2 Preheat the oven to 180°C/350°F/Gas 4. Line a bun tin (pan) with cases.

3 Using an electric mixer, beat the egg yolks with the sugar until light and creamy. Add the lemon juice and beat until well mixed. Fold in the grated mandarin rind, semolina and ground almonds using a large spoon or spatula.

4 Whisk the egg whites until stiff peaks form. Lightly stir one tablespoonful of the beaten egg white into the cake mixture to slacken the consistency, then fold in the remaining beaten egg white until just combined. Spoon into the cups until half full and bake for 15 minutes, until golden. Leave to cool on a rack.

5 For the icing, mix the ingredients, adding enough of the water to form a soft liquid icing. Spread on to the cakes. Quickly add the decorations, and leave to set.

Nutritional information per portion: Energy 346kcal/1471kJ; Protein 3.3g; Carbohydrate 82.5g, of which sugars 77.4g; Fat 2.6g, of which saturates 0.5g; Cholesterol 57mg; Calcium 53mg; Fibre 0.3g; Sodium 26mg.

Wedding cupcakes

The pink or peach sugarpaste circular toppings will stand slightly proud of the cakes, so make them a little in advance so that they firm up before they are applied with royal icing.

MAKES 12

225g/8oz marzipan
75g/3oz/6 tbsp butter, softened
100g/3½oz/scant ½ cup caster (superfine) sugar
3 eggs, lightly beaten
15ml/1 tbsp brandy
100g/3½oz/scant ½ cup ground almonds
150g/5oz/1¼ cups plain (all-purpose) flour
10ml/2 tsp baking powder

FOR THE TOPPING

450g/1lb white sugarpaste
paste food colouring in pink or peach
    and green
115g/4oz royal icing
sugarpaste flowers

1 To make the sugarpaste circles colour 175g/6oz of the sugarpaste pink or peach. Roll it out thinly on a surface dusted with icing (confectioners') sugar. Using a round crinkle-edged cutter, stamp out 12 circles and leave to dry.

2 To make the scalloped circles, roll out 140g/5oz of white sugarpaste fairly thinly. Stamp out 12 circles a little smaller than the pink circles. Leave to dry. For the leaves, colour the remaining sugarpaste green. Roll out thinly and stamp out 12 leaves. Bend them into realistic shapes and leave to dry.

3 Preheat the oven to 180°C/350°F/Gas 4. Line the cups of a muffin tin (pan) with paper cases. Mix the marzipan, butter and sugar together with an electric mixer to a smooth even paste. Leaving the motor running, add the eggs in a very thin stream, beating well until the mixture is smooth. Add the brandy and ground almonds, sift in the flour and baking powder and fold in.

4 Fill the cups three-quarters full with the cake mixture, and bake for 20–25 minutes until the cakes are golden and the centres are springy to the touch. Leave to cool in the tin for 5 minutes, then turn the cakes out on to a wire rack and leave to cool completely.

5 Use a blob of royal icing to attach the scalloped circles to the cake toppings. Brush the cakes with a little more icing and press the circles on top, then decorate with sugarpaste leaves and flowers.

Nutritional information per portion: Energy 302kcal/1269kJ; Protein 5.6g; Carbohydrate 40.4g, of which sugars 30.6g; Fat 13.7g, of which saturates 4.4g; Cholesterol 62mg; Calcium 67mg; Fibre 1.4g; Sodium 71mg.

Almond cupcakes with grapes

Bunches of marzipan grapes decorate these spectacular tea party cakes, but if you would prefer a simpler decoration you could finish the cakes elegantly with just a single green vine leaf laid on top.

MAKES 10

225g/8oz marzipan

75g/3oz/6 tbsp butter, softened

100g/3½oz/scant ½ cup caster
   (superfine) sugar

3 eggs, lightly beaten

15ml/1 tbsp grappa

100g/3½oz/scant ½ cup
   ground almonds

150g/5oz/1¼ cups plain
   (all-purpose) flour

10ml/2 tsp baking powder

10ml/2 tsp Seville orange marmalade,
   sieved (strained)

FOR THE DECORATION

500g/1¼ lb white marzipan

green and purple food colouring

50g/2oz royal icing

a little sieved (strained) apricot jam

10 dried or fresh apple stalks (optional)

1 Preheat the oven to 180°C/350°F/Gas 4. Line the cups of a bun tin (pan) with paper cases. Beat the marzipan, butter and sugar together until smooth with an electric mixer. With the whisk running, add the eggs in a very thin stream, beating well until the mixture is very smooth. Fold in the grappa, almonds and flour sifted with the baking powder. Finally, stir in the marmalade.

2 Fill the paper cases just over half full with the mixture and bake for 20 minutes until golden and springy to the touch in the centre. Leave to cool completely on a wire rack, then slice off the cake tops level with the tops of the cases.

3 Roll out 175g/6oz marzipan fairly thinly on a board dusted with icing sugar. Using a crinkle-edged cutter, cut 10 circles. Colour 115g/4oz marzipan apple green. Roll it out thinly and cut out 10 vine leaves. Colour the remaining marzipan purple and roll it into nine smooth balls for each cake.

4 Heat the jam and brush on each cake. Press on the circles of marzipan. Brush the centre of each circle with jam and stick on the grapes, then attach a vine leaf with royal icing and push in an apple stalk, if using.

Nutritional information per portion: Energy 572kcal/2404kJ; Protein 10.5g; Carbohydrate 76.9g, of which sugars 65g; Fat 25.7g, of which saturates 6.1g; Cholesterol 81mg; Calcium 122mg; Fibre 2.9g; Sodium 94mg.

Sponge cakes with frosted fruit topping

Add a pretty decoration to sponge cakes by topping them with clusters of fruits, finely crusted with sugar. Use a pretty mixture of fruits and include a few leaves and stems for a natural look.

MAKES 8–9

175g/6oz/3/4 cup butter, softened
175g/6oz/3/4 cup caster (superfine) sugar
5ml/1 tsp vanilla extract, or 5ml/
   1 tsp finely grated lemon rind
4 eggs, lightly beaten
175g/6oz/1½ cups self-raising
   (self-rising) flour, sifted

FOR THE TOPPING
Fruit, such as strawberries, seedless
   grapes, cherries, blueberries or
   redcurrants, plus a few small leaves
   and stems
1 egg white
caster (superfine) sugar

1 Preheat the oven to 180°C/350°F/Gas 4. Set 8–9 oblong silicone cake cases on a baking sheet. Place the butter and sugar in a mixing bowl. Beat together until very light and creamy. Add the vanilla or lemon rind.

2 Gradually add the eggs, beating after each addition. Add the sifted flour and fold it delicately into the mixture with a large spoon until just combined.

3 Divide the mixture among the prepared cases and bake for 20 minutes until golden brown and firm to the touch. Remove from the oven. Cool for 5 minutes, then turn out on to a wire rack to cool completely before decorating.

4 To make the topping, rinse the fruit and leaves and pat them dry with kitchen paper, as any dampness will dissolve the sugar.

5 Lightly beat the egg white until frothy. Using a brush, coat the fruit, plus stems and leaves, with the beaten egg white. Dredge with caster (superfine) sugar. Allow to dry on baking parchment. Arrange on the cakes just before serving.

Nutritional information per portion: Energy 374kcal/1568kJ; Protein 5.4g; Carbohydrate 49.3g, of which sugars 34.8g; Fat 18.6g, of which saturates 11.2g; Cholesterol 129mg; Calcium 107mg; Fibre 1.1g; Sodium 258mg.

Crystallized flower cupcakes

This traditional method of preserving summer flowers is simple to do and makes charming and very effective decorations for delicately iced cupcakes.

MAKES 10

2 eggs
115g/4oz/½ cup caster (superfine) sugar
50ml/2fl oz/¼ cup double (heavy) cream
finely grated rind of 1 lemon
115g/4oz/1 cup self-raising
   (self-rising) flour
2.5ml/½ tsp baking powder
50g/2oz/4 tbsp butter, melted

FOR THE ICING
225g/8oz/2 cups icing (confectioners') sugar
15–30ml/1–2 tbsp hot water

FOR THE DECORATION
selection of petals and/or flowers
1 egg white
50g/2oz/¼ cup caster (superfine) sugar

1 Preheat the oven to 180°C/350°F/Gas 4 and line 10 holes of a bun tin (pan) with paper cases. Beat the eggs with the sugar. Beat in the cream for 1 minute, then add the lemon rind. Sift the flour with the baking powder, then fold it lightly into the mixture, followed by the butter.

2 Three-quarters fill the paper cases with the cake mixture. Bake in the centre of the oven for 12–15 minutes until risen and golden brown. Remove from the oven and leave to cool in the bun tin for 5 minutes, then turn the cakes out on to a wire rack to cool completely.

3 To make the crystallized flowers, gather flowers when they are dry, and select clean, perfect specimens. Trim and prepare individual petals or whole flowers. Beat the egg white lightly and put it and the caster sugar in separate saucers.

4 Pick up each petal or flower and paint the entire surface, front and back, carefully with the egg white, using an artist's brush. Dredge on both sides with caster sugar so that it sticks to the egg white and coats the flower or petal. Lay the flowers and petals on baking parchment and leave them in a warm, dry place until completely dry and crisp.

5 To make the icing, sift the icing sugar into a bowl, then gradually mix in the water, a few drops at a time, beating until the mixture is the consistency of cream. Use the icing immediately to cover the cakes, while it is smooth and fluid. Before the icing dries, carefully arrange the flowers on top of the cakes.

Nutritional information per portion: Energy 608kcal/2537kJ; Protein 5.3g; Carbohydrate 59.6g, of which sugars 50.4g; Fat 40.4g, of which saturates 23.9g; Cholesterol 146mg; Calcium 89mg; Fibre 0.7g; Sodium 310mg.

Strawberry cakes

This pretty decorative design has to be assembled just before serving so that the fresh fruit doesn't discolour the sugarpaste topping. All the components can be made ahead of time though.

MAKES 10

2 eggs
115g/4oz/½ cup caster (superfine) sugar
50ml/2fl oz/¼ cup double (heavy) cream
finely grated rind of 1 lemon
115g/4oz/1 cup self-raising (self-rising) flour
2.5ml/½ tsp baking powder
50g/2oz/4 tbsp butter, melted

FOR THE DECORATION
strawberry jam
small quantity sugarpaste
pink and green food colouring
2 sizes of sugarpaste strawberry flowers
icing (confectioners') sugar, for dusting
fresh strawberries

1 Preheat the oven to 180°C/350°F/Gas 4 and line 10 holes of a bun tin (pan) with paper cases. Beat the eggs with the sugar. Beat in the cream for 1 minute, then add the lemon rind. Sift the flour with the baking powder, then fold lightly into the mixture, followed by the butter.

2 Three-quarters fill the paper cases. Bake for 15 minutes until risen and golden. Allow to cool in the tin for 5 minutes, then turn out on to a wire rack to cool.

3 Coat the top of each cake with strawberry jam. Tint some sugarpaste pink and roll out thinly on a surface dusted with icing sugar. Stamp out circles to fit the top of the cupcakes. Stick in place on top of the jam.

4 Tint another small amount of sugarpaste green. Roll out and cut out leaves and calyx shapes. Using glacé icing, stick in place. Stick a leaf in place on one side of the cupcake top. Decide where the strawberry will go and position the strawberry flowers close by. Wrap the calyx around the top of the strawberry. Use jam to hold it in place and stick on top of the cake just before serving.

Nutritional information per portion: Energy 243kcal/1024kJ; Protein 2.6g; Carbohydrate 43.4g, of which sugars 34.6g; Fat 8g, of which saturates 4.5g; Cholesterol 56mg; Calcium 42mg; Fibre 0.4g; Sodium 56mg.

Welcome to your new home cupcakes

The decoration on these cakes looks ambitious but with care the pattern is easily achieved.
You will need several piping bags with fine plain nozzles filled with different coloured royal icing.

MAKES 12

2 eggs
115g/4oz/½ cup caster (superfine) sugar
50ml/2fl oz/¼ cup double
   (heavy) cream
finely grated rind of 1 small lemon
finely grated rind of 1 small orange
115g/4oz/1 cup self-raising
   (self-rising) flour
2.5ml/½ tsp baking powder
50g/2oz/4 tbsp butter, melted

FOR THE ICING
350g/12oz/3 cups icing (confectioners')
   sugar, sifted
15ml/1 tbsp clementine or orange
   juice, strained

FOR THE DECORATION
sugarpaste coloured as desired
225g/8oz royal icing
food colouring in several shades

1 Preheat the oven to 180°C/350°F/Gas 4. Line the cups of a 12-hole bun tin (pan) with paper cases. Beat the eggs with the sugar until pale in colour. Beat in the cream, then add the grated lemon and orange rinds. Fold in the flour sifted with the baking powder, then fold in the warm melted butter.

2 Three-quarters fill the cases and bake for about 15 minutes, until golden. Leave to cool completely.

3 Roll out the sugarpaste and cut scallop edge circles to fit the cakes. Mix the icing sugar with enough fruit juice to make a thick, fluid consistency. Spread over the cakes, sticking a sugarpaste scallop on top.

4 To make the houses, tint the royal icing as desired to a soft consistency and fill several piping bags fitted with fine plain nozzles.

5 On to the sugarpaste scallop, pipe a square for the house shape. Fill with icing and smooth out any air bubbles. Add a roof and then a chimney in the same way. Pipe all the decorative details.

Nutritional information per portion: Energy 305kcal/1290kJ; Protein 2.3g; Carbohydrate 63.3g, of which sugars 56g; Fat 6.7g, of which saturates 3.8g; Cholesterol 47mg; Calcium 49mg; Fibre 0.3g; Sodium 48mg.

Teapot cupcakes

This pretty teapot cupcake is sure to be a showstopper at any party, whether it's for a child's birthday or for a young-at-heart adult. The decoration is time-consuming but worth the effort.

MAKES 10

2 eggs
115g/4oz/½ cup caster (superfine) sugar
50ml/2fl oz/¼ cup double (heavy) cream
finely grated rind of 1 lemon
115g/4oz/1 cup self-raising (self-rising) flour
2.5ml/½ tsp baking powder
50g/2oz/4 tbsp butter, melted

FOR THE DECORATION
450g/1lb sugarpaste
food pastes in pastel colours
small quantity glacé icing
icing (confectioners') sugar, for dusting

1 Preheat the oven to 180°C/350°F/Gas 4 and line 10 holes of a bun tin (pan) with paper cases. Beat the eggs with the sugar. Beat in the cream for 1 minute, then add the lemon rind. Sift the flour with the baking powder, then fold into the mixture, followed by the butter.

2 Three-quarters fill the paper cases with the cake mixture. Bake for 15 minutes until risen and golden brown. Allow to cool in the tin for 5 minutes, then turn out on to a wire rack to cool completely.

3 For the decoration, tint small quantities of sugarpaste lilac, lemon, pink and brown for each component of the teapot and teacup design. Wrap each ball separately and tightly in clear film (plastic wrap) so that it does not dry out. Keep in a cool place.

4 Coat the top of each cake with white glacé icing. Roll out some white sugarpaste and stamp out a circle using a scallop-edge cutter. Stick in place while the glacé icing is wet. Roll out a thin layer of lilac sugarpaste for the mat below the teapot. Cut a small circle using a scallop edge cutter. Impress a design in it using a modelling tool and stick in place.

5 To make the teapot, roll a ball of pale yellow paste. Make another smaller ball for the lid. Flatten the bottom edge slightly and stick in place with water. Make a small sausage for the handle and another for the spout. Fix in place with water. Carefully smooth any joins with your fingers.

6 Cut out a flat disc for the saucer. Model a bowl for the cup and fill with glacé icing to represent a drink. Make a sausage handle. The teaspoon is a small sausage rolled thinly at one end and shaped with a ball tool. The cake on the saucer is made of layered sugarpaste balls.

Nutritional information per portion: Energy 316kcal/1336kJ; Protein 3.2g; Carbohydrate 62.3g, of which sugars 53.5g; Fat 8g, of which saturates 4.5g; Cholesterol 56mg; Calcium 52mg; Fibre 0.4g; Sodium 67mg.

Autumn cupcakes

Small leaves made from rolled-out marzipan can make stunning cake decorations, used by themselves or combined with crystallized or sugarpaste flowers.

MAKES 10

2 eggs
115g/4oz/¹⁄₂ cup caster (superfine) sugar
50ml/2fl oz/¹⁄₄ cup double
    (heavy) cream
finely grated rind of 1 lemon
115g/4oz/1 cup self-raising
    (self-rising) flour
2.5ml/¹⁄₂ tsp baking powder
50g/2oz/4 tbsp butter, melted

FOR THE TOPPING
225g/8oz/2 cups icing
    (confectioners') sugar
15–30ml/1–2 tbsp hot water

FOR THE DECORATION
50g/2oz marzipan, tinted as desired

1 Preheat the oven to 180°C/350°F/ Gas 4 and line 10 holes of a bun tin (pan) with paper cases. Beat the eggs with the sugar. Beat in the cream for 1 minute, then add the lemon rind.

2 Sift the flour with the baking powder, then fold it lightly into the mixture, followed by the butter. Three-quarters fill the paper cases with the cake mixture. Bake in the centre of the oven for 15 minutes until risen and golden brown.

3 Remove from the oven and leave to cool in the bun tin for 5 minutes, then turn the cakes out on to a wire rack to cool completely.

4 To make the leaves, roll out the marzipan thinly. Cut out leaves with a cutter, or cut round a card template with a knife. Leave to dry on baking parchment. Paint the veins and edges with food colouring using a brush.

5 To make the icing, sift the icing sugar into a bowl, then gradually mix in the water, a few drops at a time, beating until the mixture is the consistency of cream.

6 Use the icing to cover the cakes, while it is smooth and fluid. Before the icing dries, carefully arrange the leaves on top of the cakes.

Nutritional information per portion: Energy 267kcal/1129kJ; Protein 2.9g; Carbohydrate 48g, of which sugars 39.2g; Fat 8.7g, of which saturates 4.6g; Cholesterol 56mg; Calcium 46mg; Fibre 0.5g; Sodium 57mg.

Halloween muffins with spooky frosting

No wonder kids love Halloween when there are treats like these to be enjoyed. These dark spicy muffins are very moist and make good use of the pumpkin flesh from the Jack-o-lanterns.

MAKES 10

100ml/3½fl oz/scant ½ cup olive oil
175g/6oz/¾ cup light muscovado
   (brown) sugar
50g/2oz/¼ cup soft dark brown sugar
1 egg, lightly beaten
7.5ml/1½ tsp vanilla extract
275g/10oz pumpkin flesh, grated
175g/6oz sultanas (golden raisins)
275g/10oz/2½ cups self-raising
   (self-rising) flour, sifted
10ml/2 tsp mixed (apple pie) spice
5ml/1 tsp ground ginger

FOR THE DECORATION

250g/9oz/2¼ cups icing (confectioners')
   sugar, sifted
5ml/1 tsp ground ginger
15ml/1 tbsp lemon juice
30ml/2 tbsp ginger syrup from a jar of
   preserved stem ginger
175g/6oz white sugarpaste

1 Preheat the oven to 180°C/350°F/Gas 4. Line the cups of a muffin tin (pan) with paper cases.

2 In a large bowl, beat the oil with the sugars. Add the egg and beat well. Stir in the vanilla extract, grated pumpkin and sultanas.

3 Sift the flour and spices into the batter and stir together until just mixed. Do not overmix.

4 Divide the batter between the paper cases. Bake for 28 minutes, or until risen and golden. Leave to set. Turn out on to a wire rack to go cold.

5 To make the ginger frosting, mix the first four ingredients together in a large bowl, then spoon over the tops of the cakes and leave to set.

6 Roll out the sugarpaste and cut out Halloween decorations. Stick them to the tops of the muffins.

Nutritional information per portion: Energy 405kcal/1718kJ; Protein 4g; Carbohydrate 85.6g, of which sugars 65g; Fat 7.6g, of which saturates 1.2g; Cholesterol 19mg; Calcium 144mg; Fibre 1.5g; Sodium 120mg.

Christmas spice cupcakes

Mincemeat, brandy and freshly ground spices are the main ingredients in these delicious celebration cupcakes, which are ideal for those who love the rich spicy flavours of Christmas.

MAKES 14

2 eggs
115g/4oz/¹⁄₂ cup golden caster
    (superfine) sugar
50ml/2fl oz/¹⁄₄ cup double (heavy) cream
grated rind of 1 clementine
115g/4oz/¹⁄₃ cup mincemeat
115g/4oz/1 cup self-raising
    (self-rising) flour
2.5ml/¹⁄₂ tsp baking powder
5ml/1 tsp mixed (apple pie) spice
10ml/2 tsp brandy
50g/2oz/4 tbsp butter, melted

FOR THE DECORATION

350g/12oz/3 cups icing (confectioners')
    sugar, sifted
15ml/1 tbsp hot water
red food colouring
175g/6oz sugarpaste

1 Preheat the oven to 180°C/350°F/Gas 4. Line the cups of a bun tin (pan) with paper cases.

2 Lightly beat the eggs with the sugar. Beat the cream into the egg mixture for about 1 minute, then add the grated clementine rind. Fold in the mincemeat. Sift in the flour, baking powder and mixed spice and fold in. Finally add the brandy and the melted butter and stir to combine.

3 Half-fill the paper cases with the batter. Place in the centre of the oven and bake for 15 minutes until risen and golden. Leave on a wire rack to cool.

4 To make the icing, mix the sugar with just enough hot water to make a soft icing. Tint one-third of it with the red food colour and spoon over four of the cakes. Ice the remaining cakes with the white icing.

5 Set aside one-third of the sugarpaste and colour the rest red. Roll both out and stamp out 10 red and 4 white snowflakes. Stick one on each cake before the icing sets.

Nutritional information per portion: Energy 272kcal/1153kJ; Protein 2g; Carbohydrate 56g, of which sugars 49.7g; Fat 6.1g, of which saturates 3.4g; Cholesterol 40mg; Calcium 43mg; Fibre 0.4g; Sodium 52mg.

Chocolate cupcakes with crème fraîche icing

These simple chocolate cakes have a sweet and sharp crème fraîche icing, which can be made using either dark or white chocolate. Cut the Christmas tree decorations out of contrasting chocolate.

MAKES 20

150g/5oz dark (bittersweet) chocolate

175ml/6fl oz/³⁄₄ cup single (light) cream

5ml/1 tsp vanilla extract

225g/8oz/1 cup golden caster (superfine) sugar

200g/7oz/scant 1 cup butter

3 eggs

225g/8oz/2 cups plain (all-purpose) flour

20g/³⁄₄oz/2 tbsp unsweetened cocoa powder

10ml/2 tsp baking powder

FOR THE ICING AND DECORATION

200g/7oz dark (bittersweet) or white chocolate

50g/2oz/4 tbsp butter

250ml/8fl oz/1 cup crème fraîche

75g/3oz/³⁄₄ cup icing (confectioners') sugar, sifted

225/8oz white or dark (bittersweet) chocolate, to decorate

1 Preheat the oven to 190°C/375°F/Gas 5. Line the cups of two bun tins (pans) with paper cases. Melt the chocolate with the cream over a low heat, stirring constantly. Stir in the vanilla and set aside.

2 Beat the sugar and butter together until light and fluffy, then beat in the eggs one at a time. Sift the flour, cocoa powder and baking powder over the butter mixture and fold in, alternating with the chocolate cream, until combined.

3 Half-fill the prepared cups and lightly smooth the tops level. Bake for 20–25 minutes, until the centres are firm. Cool on a wire rack.

4 To make the icing, melt the chocolate and butter over a pan of simmering water, stirring, until smooth. Leave to cool a little, then stir in the crème fraîche followed by the sugar. Spread the icing over the cupcakes.

5 Melt the chocolate for the trees over a pan of simmering water and pour on to a tray lined with baking parchment. Chill until just set, then cut out the shapes and chill again until firm. Stick on to the cakes.

Nutritional information per portion: Energy 419kcal/1751kJ; Protein 4.2g; Carbohydrate 43.8g, of which sugars 33.6g; Fat 26.5g, of which saturates 16.4g; Cholesterol 79mg; Calcium 57mg; Fibre 0.5g; Sodium 125mg.

Basic techniques

Cupcakes and muffins are simple to make, but some basic tips will make the process even easier. This chapter contains everything you need to know about the best ingredients and equipment to use in your baking, with basic cake recipes and suggestions for indulgent toppings and sauces. For the more confident baker, there are suggestions for delicate decorations to top your little masterpieces. With fantastic ideas for packaging and presentation, your cupcakes and muffins will make really special gifts for friends and loved ones.

Ingredients

Always use the best ingredients you can afford to buy, as their quality will give your cupcakes and muffins a really special aroma and fine flavour. They can be made from relatively few ingredients, but the addition of fruit, oats, chocolate, herbs and spices or even products such as bacon and cheese (in savoury muffins) will transform a humble cake into something even more appealing.

Flour

Different flours affect the texture and flavour of muffins as well as affecting the raising agent. Plain (all-purpose) flour is a soft, white wheat flour that has no raising agent (baking powder) added. Self-raising (self-rising) flour is the same with the addition of a raising agent. To make your own, add 5ml/ 1 tsp baking powder to every 115g/ 4oz/1 cup plain (all-purpose) flour.

RIGHT: *Bicarbonate of soda and baking powder are both raising agents used in baking.*

Self-raising flour may lose some of its raising potential if it is stored for too long: use within four months of purchase for best results. Barleycorn flour is cream-coloured and made from wheat and barley flours combined with malted barley flakes and linseed. It adds flavour, texture and fibre to muffins. Spelt flour is pale beige with a light, flavoursome wheat or nutty flavour. Light rye flour is a pale beige flour that adds a strong distinctive flavour. Some recipes use a mix of flours to add different flavours.

Baking powder

This mixture of two parts acidic cream of tartar and one part alkaline bicarbonate of soda is a raising agent. When mixed with a liquid and heated, it releases carbon dioxide, which makes cakes rise. Store it in a sealed container in a dry place because moisture will activate it. It must be mixed evenly into flour when baking: do this by sifting it twice with the flour.

Eggs

Whole beaten eggs are used for thickening cake mixtures and lightening the texture. For flavour, free range or organic eggs are the preferred choice. Large (US extra large) eggs are used in these recipes.

Butter

There is no substitute for the rich creamy taste of fresh butter. For creaming, it should be at room temperature. It is soft enough for beating when your forefinger pressed into the butter

ABOVE: *Unsalted butter produces cupcakes and muffins with a wonderfully rich flavour and warm golden colour.*

leaves a soft impression. In cold weather soften it in the microwave on low power for about 15 seconds. If you use salted butter you may not need to add the 'pinch of salt' referred to in the ingredients list in some recipes.

Buttermilk

Traditional buttermilk is the whey produced when butter is churned from cream, but nowadays it is generally

BELOW: *Use free-range, organic eggs, if possible, for the best results.*

ABOVE: *Caster sugar and granulated sugar can both be used in baking.*

made by adding acidic cultures to skimmed milk. It has a tangy off-sweet flavour, which is good in scones or muffins. Apart from balancing an over-sweet cake mixture, the acid it contains helps trigger the carbon dioxide reaction to ensure well-risen cakes.

Sugar

Caster (superfine) sugar is indispensable in cake making because its very fine crystals dissolve easily. The pale grains of organic or golden caster sugar add a light caramelized flavour. Caster (superfine) sugar is the best to use for muffins made using the creaming method because the crystals dissolve quickly. Granulated sugar has larger crystals and is ideal for cooking fruits, boiled syrups and caramel. Light soft brown sugar has a mild molasses flavour and gives a deep golden crumb. Brown sugar has no nutritional advantage over white unless specified as 'unrefined', but some people prefer the taste.

Candy sugar, or caster sugar tinted with food colouring, makes a pretty decoration sprinkled over cakes. Icing (confectioners') sugar is used for making frostings.

Flavourings

Concentrated fruit juices add flavour to frosting or syrup. Almond and vanilla extracts add intense flavour. For a coffee flavour, instant coffee granules can be diluted with a few teaspoons of hot water, but a double strength of your favourite fresh coffee is best.

Chocolate

Dark chocolate, which contains 70 per cent cocoa solids, is generally the best chocolate to use for baking. Its slightly bitter and intense chocolate flavour is not easily overshadowed by the other ingredients. Plain (semisweet) chocolate is a good choice for those

who prefer a less bitter taste. White chocolate adds sweetness to muffins, and can be marbled with dark or plain chocolate to make interesting toppings and decorations.

Dried fruit

Dates, raisins, prunes, sultanas (golden raisins) and dried apricots are frequently used in batters. Don't store dried fruit for too long; the fruits should be succulent and tender.

Fresh fruit

Use fresh fruit when it is in season. Berries, fresh figs, apples and cherries add a juiciness and natural flavour to cakes. Sharp-tasting berries such as blackcurrants or cranberries may be partly cooked in the oven first with sugar and butter before they are added to the muffin batter. Mandarins or clementines can be boiled and puréed (skin and all) to make distinctive, zesty cakes. The juice of strawberries or raspberries will colour icing pink and

ABOVE: *Chocolate is a favourite flavour to use in both cupcakes and muffins.*

ABOVE: *Mixed dried fruit is the perfect choice for breakfast muffins.*

add a lovely fruity flavour. The grated rind and juice of a lemon or orange gives a fantastic citrus lift and can balance an over-sweet cake.

Nuts

Whichever variety you choose, nuts add a distinctive flavour and texture to cake mixtures. Ground almonds are indispensable for adding a rich moistness to cakes.

Vanilla

Occasionally you may find pure vanilla bean paste (vanilla extract and beans crushed into a syrupy paste). More readily available is real vanilla extract, with a more distinct flowery aroma than essence, which is synthetic and cheaper.

Alcohol

The alcohol content of any drink you add will evaporate during baking leaving a luxurious flavour. The flavour of the alcohol you are using should complement the flavours in your cakes. Calvados (apple brandy) enhances cupcakes or muffins made with pears, apples or quince. Amaretto (almond-

ABOVE: *Raspberries are a good choice as a flavouring for simple fruit muffins.*

ABOVE: *Fruit-based spirits work particularly well in cake recipes.*

flavoured liqueur) adds to the flavour of peach, almond and apricot muffins. Marsala (fortified wine) has a special affinity with pears, chocolate and coffee. Crème de cassis (blackcurrant liqueur) is perfect for blackcurrant cakes. Sloe gin and white rum are also used. Crème de framboise (raspberry liqueur) goes well with cakes containing red berries; limoncello (lemon liqueur) suits most citrus-based cakes and grappa (an Italian aperitif made with grapes) has a special affinity with marzipan and almonds.

Cheese

Brie and soft herb and garlic cheese add a light tart flavour to savoury muffin recipes. Cheddar, Parmesan and Stilton add a strong, robust flavour.

Herbs and spices

Fresh herbs such as parsley, thyme, oregano, rosemary and garlic add aroma and flavour to baking. All herbs should be finely chopped before you

ABOVE: *Ginger and other spices will give your cupcakes and muffins a kick.*

add them to the recipe. Spices commonly used in baking include cinnamon, ginger, nutmeg and mixed (apple pie) spice. Whole spices, freshly ground, deliver the finest flavour and will last longer if they are stored in a sealed container away from light. Spices bought ready ground will last for up to 6 months.

Vegetables

Versatile ingredients in muffins, these should be finely grated before they are added to the batter. Use courgettes (zucchini), marrow (large zucchini), pumpkin, squash, onions, carrots, beetroot (beet) and sweet potato for sweet and savoury flavours.

Food colouring

Use liquid food colouring for glacé icing unless a very rich colour is required, when you should use a paste. Always use paste for colouring sugarpaste to preserve its firm consistency. Add just a tiny amount.

ABOVE: *Icing can be tinted with food colouring or bought ready-coloured.*

Royal icing

This type of icing sets hard, and is good for attaching sugarpaste decorations. Sift 250g/9oz/2¼ cups icing (confectioners') sugar into a bowl and make a well in the centre. Add 1 egg white, lightly beaten, and 15ml/1 tbsp lemon juice; whisk until stiff and glossy.

Sugarpaste (rolled fondant)

This is good for making decorations as it is easily sculpted or rolled and shaped with cutters. You can make your own, but ready-made sugarpaste is of excellent quality. Keep it well wrapped as it dries very quickly. Coloured sugarpastes are available, and are useful if you require a very strong colour. Otherwise, it is more practical to tint the paste with a small amount of food colouring paste.

Condensed milk

This is a skimmed milk that is condensed by various stages of boiling until it is thick and creamy with a delicious sticky texture. To enrich it further, cans may be boiled in a pan of boiling water for several hours to produce a dense amber-coloured caramel, known as dulce de leche (also available ready-made.)

Cornmeal (polenta)

Made from ground corn, the texture of cornmeal can be coarse or fine. Choose finely ground for baking.

Cream

Fresh whipped double (heavy) cream needs sweetening to balance the sweetness of the cake, and can be flavoured with vanilla, caramel, coffee, chocolate, lemon curd or fruit liqueurs. Avoid over-whipping double cream, as it can separate when it is piped.

Crème fraîche

This cream has a delicate sourness that works very well as a topping on sweeter cakes. It can be flavoured in the same way as cream. The delicate sourness of crème fraîche contrasts well with warm melted chocolate for a simple, yet delicious, cake topping.

Bran

Made from the outer layer of cereal, such as the husks of wheat or oats, bran is a natural product valued for its fibre content. It adds flavour and texture to muffin batters.

Maple syrup

Maple syrup is graded according to colour and strength of flavour. Like honey it can be used in place of sugar to add sweetness to mixtures for cupcakes or muffins.

Jam

To make a jam glaze, simmer together 45ml/3 tbsp sieved apricot jam, 15–30ml/1–2 tbsp water and 30ml/2 tbsp sugar until thickened. This can be brushed over cakes or fruit toppings to add gloss and extra flavour, or used to glue marzipan to the cake tops. Quince jam glaze, made in the same way, is suitable for cakes baked with quince slices, apples or pears; redcurrant jelly glaze will enhance red berries.

Rose or orange flower water

The heady scents of roses and orange blossom are distilled into bottles for use in cooking. One teaspoon of a pure extract is sufficient to add fragrance to about 12 small cakes.

ABOVE: *Fruit jams can be used to make a simple glaze for cakes.*

Equipment

Although it is possible to make do with a few multi-purpose kitchen utensils, it is better to invest in quality equipment if you intend to bake cupcakes and muffins on a regular basis. An interesting selection of small decorative moulds, cutters and interesting paper liners will add an extra creative dimension to your cakes and make them visually memorable.

Paper cake cases
Finely pleated cake papers are convenient for easy release from the tins (pans) and help to keep the cakes fresher. They also make an attractive decorations too as are

ABOVE: *Use paper cake cases to line muffin tins. Paper and foil cases are made in a range of sizes, colours and patterns.*

RIGHT: *Muffin and bun tins are essential pieces of equipment.*

available in a variety of colours and patterns. Make sure they are non-stick or most of the cake will stick to the paper. Use the cases double for neater cakes, and in the absence of a muffin tin treble the paper cases (one inserted inside the other) and bake the muffins or cakes free-standing on a baking sheet in the oven. Dariole moulds or tall, slim muffin tins are lined with pleated cake cases cut to size from paper liners used for loaf tins.

Muffin and bun tins (pans)
These can be made of metal or silicone rubber. Silicone has a controlled flexibility that makes it easy to release the cakes. Muffin cups are usually taller and straighter than bun cups, which have sloping sides. Individual dariole moulds are used to make tall, slim muffins.

Baking parchment
This can be used for lining the muffin tins (pans) or terracotta pots, or for cutting little paper collars for the muffins after baking. Non-stick siliconized baking parchment is useful for inter-leaving cakes and decorations in storage boxes. Silicone

paper can also be used to make flat iced shapes to be applied to the top of cakes after they are dry.

Baking tins (pans)
A small shallow baking tin is required in some of the recipes for baking fruit with sugar and jam.

Canelle knife
This is a type of zester that cuts fine spaghetti-like strands from hard-skinned citrus fruits. Use the strands to decorate the tops of lemon- or orange-flavoured cakes.

Flowerpots
Small, heat-resistant terracotta flowerpots, available from good kitchenware shops (rather than

those from garden centres, which have a drainage hole in the base), make attractive baking containers for unusual-looking muffins. Make sure that you grease them well before you add the lining paper, or you may have trouble releasing muffins from the mould when they come out of the oven.

Ovenproof china cups

These make unusual baking receptacles for muffins. They are available from specialist cookware shops, or online. Choose medium-sized cups with a 175ml/6fl oz/ $^3/_4$ cup capacity, which is the perfect size to line with a standard paper case. Alternatively, china cups make an attractive holder in which to present muffins in paper cases.

ABOVE: *Cupcakes and muffins can be baked in different containers, depending on the occasion.*

Grater

A box cheese grater is perfect for grating hard cheese as well as a variety of vegetables, such as carrots or courgettes. Grated chocolate is also used in some cake recipes. For best results, chill the chocolate overnight in the refrigerator before you grate it.

LEFT: *A box cheese grater can also be used to grate chilled chocolate or vegetables.*

ABOVE: *Different-sized measuring spoons should be used for fine ingredients.*

ABOVE: *An electric whisk will take some of the hard work out of mixing ingredients together.*

Kitchen scissors

Keep a pair of kitchen scissors in your working area and use them specifically for culinary purposes, such as snipping bacon and fresh herbs into muffin batters and, of course, cutting paper liners.

Hand-held electric whisk

These are useful for making quick buttercream and whipped cream. This can also be done by hand, but is time-consuming. An electric whisk can also be used in a pan over heat for meringue-based recipes.

Measuring spoons

Exact spoon measurements are vital, particularly for baking powder, vanilla extract, spices, orange and rose waters. Level off the top of each filled cup with the back of a knife for an accurate quantity of a dry mix ingredient.

Knives

A palette knife is ideal for smoothing buttercream and frostings over the tops of cakes and muffins. A sharp-pointed knife is useful for cutting shapes around paper templates when cutting from cookie dough.

Spoons

As well as a set of measuring spoons for fine ingredients, a large metal spoon is efficient for folding in dry and wet ingredients, without losing air from the batter. Wooden spoons are also useful for beating ingredients together.

Sieve (strainer)

Essential for sifting flour and raising agents together, and for sifting icing (confectioners') sugar when making smooth icing or buttercream. Have

ABOVE: *Many different-shaped cutters are available from cookware suppliers. Use them to decorate the tops of cupcakes.*

ABOVE: *Dredgers have a fine gauze and are good for adding a final dusting of icing sugar to finished cakes.*

at least two – one for dry ingredients and another for wet ones. Use a tea strainer to sift coffee granules.

Decorative cutters

A graded set of plain and scalloped cutters is used in some of the recipes. Dip them into icing sugar to prevent the sugarpaste or marzipan sticking to them when you stamp out circles for the tops of cupcakes. Choose good quality steel cutters for accurate circles – blunt ones will compress the edges. Shaped cutters – leaves, flowers, rabbits, Christmas trees, letters and numerals – are useful. Plunger cutters are particularly good for producing really professional-looking flowers and leaf shapes with detailed veins. They are available

LEFT: *An electric food mixer is useful for beating together butter and sugar.*

from specialist sugarcraft shops, some good cookware suppliers, and from online retailers.

Dredger

This is a metal container with a fine gauze lid in which you can store icing sugar. Use it to dust the work surface when working with marzipan and rolled sugarpaste. Because it has a finer gauze than a kitchen sieve it is better for adding a fine last-minute dusting of icing sugar or cocoa powder.

Electric food mixer

For time-saving and convenience, electric food mixers are great for beating together butter and sugar, and for beating eggs. However, it is advisable to fold in the dry ingredients by hand. Some electric mixers have a liquidizer attachment – these can be very useful for making fruit purées.

Moulds

These are used to form small pieces of coloured marzipan or sugarpaste into intricate shapes to use for cake decorations. Look out for small antique chocolate moulds, decorative wooden fabric printing stamps, or wooden butter moulds for embossing your cupcake or muffin toppings.

Stencils and templates

You can buy these ready-made, but it is also quite easy to cut out your own simple shapes, such as birds, stars and flowers, from heavy duty tracing paper or thin cardboard. These are useful if you want to make sure your decorations look exactly the same on each cake.

Weighing scales

It is well worth investing in a good set of kitchen scales which are able to weigh small or large quantities with precision. Use either imperial or metric measurements, never a combination.

ABOVE: *A pastry brush will come in useful for applying glazes to the tops of your cupcakes and muffins.*

Wire racks

These are essential to allow the steam to escape easily from the hot cakes. A circular wire rack can also be used as a stencil to make a spider's web pattern if placed over the top of a cake and sprinkled with a dusting of icing sugar. Use the rack of a grill (broiler) pan as a surface on which to cool cakes, if you like.

Pastry brush

Look out for wide, soft brushes that will cover the whole surface of a cupcake in one sweep when adding a hot jam glaze or brushing over royal icing as a fixing agent for toppings. You will also need a smaller artist's brush for sticking on decorations.

LEFT: *Mixing bowls of different sizes are useful for baking.*

ABOVE: *Use a good set of weighing scales for accuracy. Use imperial or metric measurements, not a mixture.*

Piping (pastry) bags

These are essential for piping buttercreams and other creamy frostings; large piping bags are usually made from fabric and fitted with large plastic nozzles that can easily be washed, dried and reused. Ready-made, disposable piping bags made of baking parchment are used for piping thin lines for small decorations. Snip off the merest tip of the bag for an instant nozzle.

Mixing bowls

Choose a selection of mixing bowls that fit inside one another. Many are attractive enough to sit out on the kitchen surface, close to hand, rather than be packed away in a cupboard. A set of small bowls is handy for small quantities of ingredients, or for separating eggs.

Basic recipes

Most of the recipes in this book are based on these basic recipes, with the addition of different ingredients chosen for their flavours or texture. There are two ways to make a basic cupcake – the creamed method and the melting method. Recipes for a basic sweet muffin and a basic savoury muffin are included, as well as a time-saving way of pre-preparing a basic dry mix to store and then add to wet ingredients when needed.

CUPCAKES

The two methods of making cupcakes will produce different results, so choose the one which is most suited to your recipe.

Creamed method

The butter is beaten with the sugar until creamy, then combined with the flour and flavourings. The resulting cake has a moist, dense crumb. Use a wooden spoon or an electric mixer – the latter is less time-consuming.

MAKES 8–9
175g/6oz/3/4 cup butter, softened
175g/6oz/3/4 cup caster
   (superfine) sugar
5ml/1 tsp vanilla extract, or 5ml/1 tsp
   finely grated lemon rind
4 eggs, lightly beaten
175g/6oz/1 1/2 cups self-raising
   (self-rising) flour, sifted

1 Preheat the oven to 180°C/ 350°F/Gas 4. Line 8–9 cups of a bun tin (pan) with paper cases.

2 Place the butter and sugar in a large mixing bowl. Beat together with a wooden spoon or an electric mixer until the mixture is very light and creamy.

3 Next add the vanilla extract or grated lemon rind for flavour.

4 Gradually add the eggs to the bowl, beating the mixture well after each addition.

5 Next add the sifted flour to the bowl and fold it delicately into the mixture with a large wooden spoon until it is just combined. Do not overmix.

6 Divide the mixture among the paper cases, filling them about three-quarters full, and bake for 20 minutes until the cakes are golden brown and the centres feel firm to the touch. Remove from the oven.

7 Leave to cool for 5 minutes, then turn out on to a wire rack to cool completely before icing and decorating.

Melting method

Here the butter is melted and left to cool slightly. The remaining cake ingredients are combined, and the cooled, melted butter is beaten in last. The resulting cakes will have a soft sponge-like texture and will rise evenly to give a flat top suitable for glacé icing and sugarpaste toppings.

MAKES 10
2 eggs
115g/4oz/1/2 cup caster
   (superfine) sugar
50ml/2fl oz/1/4 cup double
   (heavy) cream
finely grated rind of 1 lemon
115g/4oz/1 cup self-raising
   (self-rising) flour
2.5ml/1/2 tsp baking powder
50g/2oz/4 tbsp butter, melted

1 Preheat the oven to 180°C/350°F/Gas 4 and line 10 holes of a bun tin (pan) with paper cases.

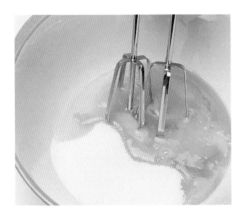

2 Beat the eggs with the sugar using an electric mixer. Beat in the cream for 1 minute, then add the lemon rind.

3 Sift the flour with the baking powder, then fold it into the mixture, followed by the melted butter.

4 Three-quarters fill the paper cases with the cake mixture.

5 Bake in the centre of the oven for 12–15 minutes until risen and golden brown. Test by lightly pressing the centres of the cakes with your fingers: the sponge should lightly spring back.

6 Remove from the oven and leave to cool and set in the bun tin for 5 minutes, then turn the cakes out on to a wire rack. Allow them to cool completely before icing and decorating them.

MUFFINS

A simple muffin batter is easy to make and can be flavoured with either sweet or savoury ingredients.

Basic sweet muffin

A basic sweet batter can be enhanced with many different flavours, but fresh fruit is the simplest. Raspberries are used here but you could try fresh apricots, blueberries, blackcurrants or figs, cut into bitesize pieces. Serve warm, lightly dusted with icing (confectioners') sugar, if you like.

MAKES 7–8 STANDARD MUFFINS
For the basic sweet muffin
225g/8oz/2 cups plain (all-purpose) flour
12.5ml/2 rounded tsp baking powder
150g/5oz/¾ cup golden caster (superfine) sugar
75g/3oz/6 tbsp butter, melted
2.5ml/½ tsp vanilla extract
1 egg, lightly beaten
200ml/7fl oz/scant 1 cup buttermilk

FOR FLAVOURING
150g/5oz/scant 1 cup raspberries
15ml/1 tbsp caster (superfine) sugar (optional)

1 Preheat the oven to 180°C/350°F/Gas 4. Grease the cups of a muffin tin (pan) or line with paper cases.

2 If you are using berries that are too tart for your taste, arrange the fruit in a single layer on a plate and sprinkle with 15ml/1 tbsp sugar. Set aside.

3 To make the batter, sift the dry ingredients into a mixing bowl and form a well in the centre.

4 In a separate bowl, mix the melted butter, vanilla extract, egg and buttermilk together. Pour into the dry ingredients then fold partly together.

5 Lightly combine half of the fruit and any syrup into the batter. Spoon the mixture into the prepared paper cases and sprinkle the remaining fruit on top.

6 Bake the muffins for 25 minutes, until they look golden and well risen and are springy to the touch.

7 Leave to cool and set slightly in the tin, then transfer them from the tin to a wire rack to cool. Serve fresh, or store in an airtight container for up to 3 days.

Calculating quantities
• For 8 muffins weigh half of the basic dry mix and flavouring (650g/1¹/₂lb) into a mixing bowl. Mix lightly with 2 eggs and 200ml/7fl oz/scant 1 cup buttermilk.
• For 4 muffins weigh a quarter of the quantity of basic dry mix (350g/ 12oz) and flavouring into a mixing bowl. Mix lightly with 1 egg and 100ml/3¹/₂fl oz/ scant ¹/₂ cup buttermilk.
• For 2 muffins weigh 175g/6oz of the basic dry mix and flavouring into a bowl. Mix with ¹/₂ egg and 50ml/2fl oz/¹/₄ cup buttermilk. Spoon the batter into paper cases and bake for 25 minutes until risen and cooked through.

Basic savoury muffin

This basic recipe has many variations. Here a soft herb cream cheese and buttermilk are the basis for the 'savoury' flavour, while bacon adds extra saltiness. Eat savoury muffins fresh for the best flavour. Store in an airtight container for up to three days.

MAKES 7 LARGE MUFFINS

For the basic savoury muffin
225g/8oz/2 cups self-raising (self-rising) flour
10ml/2 tsp baking powder
10ml/2 tsp maple syrup or caster (superfine) sugar
1 egg
75g/3oz/6 tbsp butter, melted
115g/4oz/¹/₂ cup soft garlic and herb cream cheese
175ml/6fl oz/³/₄ cup buttermilk

FOR FLAVOURING
30ml/2 tbsp olive oil, for frying
15g/¹/₂ oz/1 tbsp butter, for frying
225g/8oz very lean smoked bacon, plus extra to serve
maple syrup, to serve

1 Preheat the oven to 180°C/ 350°F/Gas 4. Line the cups of a muffin tin (pan) with paper cases.

2 Carefully sift the flour, baking powder and sugar, but not the maple syrup, into a large bowl. Make a well in the centre.

3 Beat the egg, butter, cream cheese and buttermilk together in a bowl with the maple syrup, if using.

4 In a frying pan, heat the oil and butter over a medium heat and fry all the bacon, until it is lightly caramelized. This should take about about 4 minutes.

5 Remove the pan from the heat. Allow to cool slightly, then cut the bacon into tiny pieces and set aside a small quantity for serving.

6 Pour the wet ingredients into the well in the dry ingredients.

7 Add the bacon and any juices from the pan. Mix until combined.

8 Spoon the batter into the paper cases and bake for 25–30 minutes, until the muffins are golden.

9 Leave to cool slightly, then serve the muffins warm, topped with extra bacon. Drizzle over warm maple syrup.

Canadian muffin mix

A mix of semi-prepared ingredients can be kept in an airtight container in the refrigerator, ready to make muffins. You will need to use one quantity of basic dry mix, and one quantity of wet ingredients. The flavourings can vary. Eat fresh for best taste, or store in an airtight container for three days.

MAKES 16 STANDARD MUFFINS
For the basic dry mix
450g/1lb/4 cups plain
   (all-purpose) flour
175g/6oz/3/4 cup butter, diced
30ml/2 tbsp baking powder
pinch of salt
275g/10oz/11/3 cups caster
   (superfine) sugar

FOR FLAVOURING
75g/3oz/3/4 cup pecans, roughly
   chopped
rind of 1 large orange, finely grated
50g/2oz/4 tbsp sesame seeds
275g/10oz/11/3 cups dried
   mixed berries

FOR THE WET INGREDIENTS
4 eggs
400ml/14fl oz/12/3 cups buttermilk

1 Sift the flour into a large mixing bowl. Add the butter and rub it into the flour to form very fine breadcrumbs. Ensure that the butter has a long shelf-life.

2 Sift the baking powder, salt and sugar into the flour and butter mixture, then add the flavouring ingredients. Stir well to combine.

3 Transfer the contents to an airtight container and store in the refrigerator for up to 1 month.

4 Preheat the oven to 180°C/350°F/ Gas 4. As a change from paper cases, cut baking parchment into 12.5cm/5in squares and press into the greased cups of a muffin tin (pan).

5 Decant the dry muffin mix into a mixing bowl. Stir in the wet ingredients, until just combined.

6 Spoon the batter into the paper cases until almost full and bake for 25 minutes, until a skewer inserted into the centre comes out clean.

7 Leave to set in the tin for a few minutes before turning out to cool.

Toppings and sauces

Coloured or flavoured, or simply an elegant white, frosting is part of what makes cupcakes so appealing. While muffins are often left undecorated, serving them with an indulgent fruity sauce on the side can really add that special touch. All of these recipes can be used for cupcakes and muffins.

GLACÉ ICING

Also known as water icing, this is the simplest of all icing recipes, and is ideal for decorating small cakes. It's quick to mix, with only two basic ingredients, and provided you take care to get the consistency right it flows easily over the surface and sets to a glossy smoothness.

Glacé icing, made with finely sifted icing (confectioners') sugar and hot water, makes a basic topping that is suitable for many cakes. The icing can be flavoured with vanilla, fruit juice and zest, chocolate, coffee or alcohol, and looks wonderful in delicate, pastel colours. It is important to get the consistency exactly right: too thick and it will not form a super-smooth glossy coating; too thin and it will run over the top and down the sides of the cake. Glacé icing sets to form a crisp surface, but never becomes rock hard. The consistency determines how many cakes the icing covers.

MAKES ENOUGH FOR 16 CUPCAKES
225g/8oz/2 cups icing (confectioners') sugar
15–30ml/1–2 tbsp hot water
a few drops of food colouring (optional)

1 First, carefully sift the icing sugar into a large mixing bowl.

2 Gradually mix in the hot water, a few drops at a time, beating well until the mixture is the consistency of cream.

3 Add one or two drops of food colouring to the mixture (with caution). For a more vibrant colour use paste food colouring, available from specialist suppliers. Stir well until evenly coloured. Alternatively, leave the icing white.

4 Use the icing immediately, while it is smooth and fluid. Add any further decoration before the icing dries.

Icing variations

Try these different ideas for interesting ways to liven up the toppings for your cakes.

Fresh fruit flavouring The strained juice from fresh berries such as raspberries, redcurrants or citrus fruits can be used to scent and softly colour plain icing and glazes. A more concentrated citrus hit can be achieved by adding finely grated rind or replacing some of the water used to make up the glacé icing with fruit juice.

Melting liqueur fondant Lift the flavour of icing with 15–30ml/1–2 tbsp crème de framboise (raspberry liqueur), limoncello (lemon liqueur), or another fruit-based liqueur, which will add fruity tones.

Iced fruit Small bunches of redcurrants or cherries (with their stalks left on) dipped in melting liqueur fondant and left to set on baking parchment make a very appealing and seasonal topping for summer cakes.

BUTTERCREAM

A clear favourite for filling and decorating sponge cakes, the rich sweet taste of buttercream will complement the plainest of cupcakes and muffins, and the basic recipe can be flavoured with almost anything you choose. Add food colouring to buttercream, if you like, to complement your cakes' flavours and decorations.

Vanilla buttercream

This classic recipe for vanilla buttercream makes a delicious frosting that can easily be spread, piped or textured.

FOR 8–9 CUPCAKES

75g/3oz/6 tbsp butter, softened

175g/6oz/1½ cups icing (confectioners') sugar, double sifted, plus extra for dusting

½ vanilla pod (bean), split, or a few drops of vanilla extract

food colouring (optional)

1 To make buttercream, use butter that has had time to reach room temperature. Beat it well before beating in the sifted icing sugar. Ensure that no lumps remain.

2 Split the vanilla pod in half and scrape out the seeds. Mix the seeds into the buttercream (or add few drops of vanilla extract). Add food colouring if desired. Spread on to cakes.

Pink raspberry buttercream

This is perfect for decorating raspberry or plain buttermilk muffins.

FOR DECORATING 8 CAKES

175g/6oz/¾ cup butter, softened

350g/12oz/3 cups icing (confectioners') sugar, sifted

20ml/4tsp lemon juice

25ml/1½ tbsp raspberry jam, sieved (strained)

1 or 2 drops red food colouring (optional)

1 Beat the butter with the icing sugar until smooth and fluffy. Stir in the lemon juice and sieved jam.

2 Add a few drops of food colouring and stir until the buttercream is evenly coloured and a soft consistency.

3 Transfer the buttercream into a piping bag and use to decorate cakes.

Buttercream tips

• The icing will keep for up to three days in an airtight container stored in a refrigerator.

• Buttercream can be coloured with paste colours. Add a little at a time using a cocktail stick (toothpick) until you reach the desired shade.

• You can apply buttercream with a knife and make a smooth finish, or you can pipe the icing on to your cupcakes or muffins using a plain or fluted nozzle, or use a serrated scraper for a ridged finish.

Buttercream flavourings

The basic buttercream recipe can be flavoured with just about anything you want, but try these ideas for starters:

• **White chocolate** Melt 350g/ 12oz white chocolate and allow to cool slightly. Add this to the icing with the vanilla extract.

• **Coffee** Stir 10ml/2 tsp instant coffee into 15ml/1 tbsp boiling water. Allow to cool before beating into the icing.

• **Mocha** Stir 5ml/1 tsp cocoa powder into 10ml/2 tsp boiling water. Allow to cool before beating into the icing. Add a few drops of coffee extract.

• **Orange, lemon or lime** Use orange, lemon or lime juice instead of the vanilla extract, and add 10ml/2tsp finely grated citrus rind. Omit the rind if using the icing for piping. Lightly tint the icing with food colouring, if you like.

• **Peanut butter** In addition to the vanilla extract add 140g/ 5oz/²⁄₃ cup peanut butter to the buttercream mixture.

Chocolate buttercream

This rich chocolatey buttercream makes an indulgent topping for chocolate cupcakes or chocolate chip muffins.

MAKES ENOUGH TO COVER 6 CUPCAKES

75g/3oz/6 tbsp unsalted butter or margarine, softened

175g/6oz/1¹⁄₂ cups icing (confectioners') sugar, sifted

15ml/1 tbsp unsweetened cocoa powder

2.5ml/¹⁄₂ tsp vanilla extract

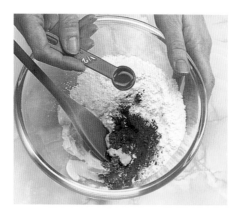

1 Place the softened butter, icing sugar and cocoa powder in a large mixing bowl. Add the vanilla extract.

2 Beat the ingredients together thoroughly, using a wooden spoon or an electric mixer.

OTHER TOPPINGS AND SAUCES

In addition to glacé icing and buttercream, there are a whole host of other flavoured toppings that are perfect for giving your cupcakes and muffins that finishing touch. The possibilities are endless, but try these recipes for starters.

American cream cheese frosting

Don't confine this famous cream cheese buttercream to spicy carrot cake. It also makes a splendid topping for fudgy chocolate or ginger cakes.

MAKES ENOUGH TO COVER 12 CUPCAKES

140g/5oz/10 tbsp butter, softened

225g/8oz/1 cup cream cheese

225–250g/8–9oz/2–2¹⁄₄ cups icing (confectioners') sugar, sifted

5ml/1 tsp finely grated lemon rind

1 Beat the butter and cream cheese together until soft and creamy.

2 Gradually beat in the icing sugar until the mixture is smooth, with a spreadable consistency that holds a soft peak. Mix in the grated lemon rind.

Luxurious vanilla cream

This is a light, ultra-smooth topping for a special occasion.

MAKES ENOUGH TO COVER 8 CUPCAKES

175g/6oz/¾ cup caster (superfine) sugar

3 egg whites

175g/6oz/¾ cup butter, softened

½ vanilla pod (bean), split

1 Put 45ml/3 tbsp water into a pan with the sugar and heat gently until dissolved. Bring to the boil and boil until it reaches 121°C/250°F (measure with a jam thermometer). Remove from the heat.

2 Beat the egg whites until the mixture holds its shape in peaks.

3 Pour the syrup in a thin steady stream over the egg whites, whisking constantly at a low speed. until the meringue is thick and cold (about 10–15 minutes), then set aside.

4 In a separate bowl, beat the butter until it is creamy. Gradually add the meringue a large spoonful at a time with the vanilla seeds, whisking well after each addition.

Butterscotch frosting

Soft light brown sugar and treacle make a rich and tempting frosting.

MAKES ENOUGH TO COVER 6 CUPCAKES

75g/3oz/6 tbsp unsalted butter, softened

45ml/3 tbsp milk

25g/1oz/2 tbsp soft light brown sugar

15ml/1 tbsp black treacle (molasses)

350g/12oz/3 cups icing (confectioners') sugar, sifted

1 Place the butter, milk, brown sugar and treacle in a bowl over a pan of simmering water. Stir until the butter melts and the sugar dissolves completely.

2 Remove from the heat and stir in the icing sugar. Cool before using.

Chocolate ganache

This recipe can be used to make a topping, or to make truffles.

MAKES ENOUGH TO COVER 25 CUPCAKES

150ml/¼ pint/⅔ cup double (heavy) cream

350g/12oz dark or plain (bittersweet or semisweet) chocolate

50g/2oz/4 tbsp butter

1 Bring the cream to the boil. Remove from the heat and leave for 1 minute. Break the chocolate into the hot cream. Stir until the chocolate melts and the mixture is smooth.

2 Add the butter and stir until the mixture is glossy. Use immediately for a topping. To make truffles, chill, shape and toss in cocoa powder.

Warm caramel sauce

This sauce keeps in a covered bowl in the refrigerator. Warm it through before using it to regain its light flowing consistency.

**MAKES ENOUGH TO COAT
8 MUFFINS**
275g/10oz/1½ cups caster
    (superfine) sugar
150ml/10 tbsp crème fraîche or double
    (heavy) cream

1 Put the sugar in a pan with 150ml/10 tbsp water and simmer gently over a medium heat, stirring continuously until dissolved. Bring to the boil until it turns golden.

2 Remove from the heat and plunge the base of the pan in a bowl of cold water for a few seconds to arrest the cooking.

3 Stir in the cream. If the caramel stiffens, replace the pan over a low to medium heat and stir until it is smooth and glossy. Serve warm, or reheat gently if necessary.

4 Allow to go cold before refrigerating for up to 1 week in a sealed container.

Quick blueberry jam

Spoon blueberry jam and plain (natural) yogurt over blueberry or berry brioche muffins, or a recipe with spices, apples or nuts. This delicious jam also adds a sweet note to more substantial healthy bran muffins.

MAKES 450G/1LB
350g/12oz/3 cups blueberries
200g/7oz/1 cup caster (superfine) sugar
thin 5cm/2in strip of lemon peel

1 Put the blueberries in a heavy pan with 50ml/2fl oz/¼ cup water. Bring to the boil, then simmer for 5 minutes, until the berries burst, stirring occasionally.

2 Add the sugar and lemon peel, then stir in gently and continue to stir until the sugar dissolves.

3 Boil for 7 minutes, or until the jam thickens, stirring occasionally.

4 Pour the hot jam into clean, sterilized and warmed glass jars. Seal and leave to go cold. Store in the refrigerator for up to 1 month. Serve with breakfast muffins, on the side, or spooned over the top.

Passion fruit and lime curd

Eat this fruity sauce with warm citrus muffins and serve with a spoonful of yogurt.

MAKES 450G/1LB
30ml/2 tbsp juice and grated rind of
    1 lime
115g/4oz/½ cup butter
175g/6oz/¾ cup caster
    (superfine) sugar
1 egg, plus 3 yolks
3–4 passion fruit

1 Put the lime juice and rind, butter and sugar in a medium pan. Lightly beat the egg with the egg yolks and add to the pan.

2 Add the passion fruit. Stir over a medium heat until thick. Pour into a glass jar. Seal. Chill for up to 1 month.

Decorations

The possibilities for decorating cupcakes and muffins are just about endless! Sugarpaste and marzipan are both extremely versatile and can be made into whatever shape you can think of. Chocolate can be melted and made into different shapes, while fresh flowers, sweets and marshmallows make more unusual decorations.

WORKING WITH SUGARPASTE

A versatile medium for all kinds of edible ornaments, sugarpaste can be rolled out like pastry and used to cover cakes of all sizes with a perfect, smooth, sweet coating. It can also be stamped, embossed and moulded to make a wonderful range of three-dimensional decorations.

Sugarpaste, also known as fondant, is a combination of liquid glucose, gelatine, glycerine and icing (confectioners') sugar, and can be bought ready-made. You can make it at home, but the availability of some excellent products on the market means it is more convenient to buy it. Sugarpaste is sold vacuum packed in plastic bags. When you use it make sure that during and after use you keep it well wrapped with plastic wrap, or it will become dry and chalky in texture and unusable. If the paste is too sticky, add a little finely sifted icing sugar to it.

Cutting sugarpaste shapes

Once you have tinted your sugarpaste, it can be rolled out flat and cut into shapes. Flowers, birds, animals, lettering – let your imagination go wild!

1 Lightly dust a chopping board with sifted icing sugar. Roll out a small amount of coloured sugarpaste. For a multi-coloured effect, use balls of different coloured sugarpaste and press them together before rolling.

2 Cut out simple shapes – like this fish design – freehand, using a sharp knife and taking care.

3 For more complex designs, make (or buy) a template from light card. This method is useful when a recipe requires the same shape several times.

4 Lay the template on top of the rolled-out sugarpaste, hold in place with one hand, and carefully cut out the shape with the other hand.

Tinting sugarpaste

Subtle tones of sugarpaste often look much more appealing than bright ones, especially if the cakes are for an elegant celebration. If you require a vibrant colour it is better to buy it ready coloured from a sugarcraft shop, because the quantities of colour needed make the paste too wet.

1 To colour sugarpaste add a few drops of food colour or a few specks of paste to a ball of sugarpaste.

2 Knead until the colour is evenly distributed throughout the sugarpaste.

Moulding sugarpaste shapes

Plastic moulds are a good investment. The texture of sugarpaste makes it ideal for shaping decorative moulds.

1 Place the paste on a working surface lightly dusted with sifted icing sugar, and knead until it is smooth and free from cracks. Colour it as required.

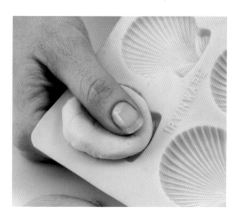

2 Divide the paste into portions and press each into a decorative mould. Press repeatedly to ensure the paste adheres. Trim the top so that it is smooth and level.

3 Chill for several hours. Press the tip of a knife between the paste and the mould to create an air pocket. Prise out the shape and leave to defrost. Smooth out any knife marks once the sugarpaste has softened sufficiently.

Making plunger-cut flowers

With a plunger cutter, you can make perfect shapes. The plunge mechanism in each cutter pushes the shape out of the cutter and makes it cupped.

1 Lightly dust the work surface with sifted icing sugar. Roll out a small ball of coloured sugarpaste to 3mm/⅛in thick using a small rolling pin.

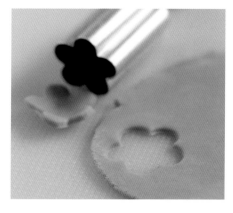

2 Use a plunger cutter (available in different shapes) to cut out flowers and lift them gently from the surface using a flat palette knife or metal spatula to avoid squashing the edges of the petals with your fingers.

3 Using a fine plain nozzle and a small quantity of royal icing in a piping bag, pipe a small blob at the centre of each flower.

Stamping sugarpaste

Use different-shaped cutters to create delicate and intricate decorations for your cupcakes and muffins. The stamps can be found at specialist cookware stores, or online, and are available in a wide variety of different shapes and sizes.

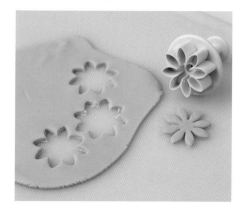

1 Roll out a small ball of coloured fondant on a light dusting of icing sugar to 3mm/⅛ in thick and cut out each shape.

2 Use a ball modelling tool to manipulate sugarpaste flowers into a cup shape, bending the petals up a little. Pipe the centre and add false stamens if you like. Use a little royal icing or egg white to attach to cool, iced cupcakes.

Embossing sugarpaste

Imprint patterns in soft sugarpaste with decorative tools.

1 Use a decorative rolling pin or craft stamp, available from sugarcraft shops, and press firmly on to thinly rolled out paste to leave an imprint. Remove with care.

2 Use a cookie cutter to cut out the desired shape. Stick to the top of a cupcake with a little royal icing. This works best on cakes with flat tops.

Making sugarpaste roses

The icing used to make these simple yet effective flowers should be delicately tinted in pale colours, such as pink or yellow. It can also be scented with a little rose water for an extra-feminine touch.

1 Tint a small amount of sugarpaste pink and roll out very thinly.

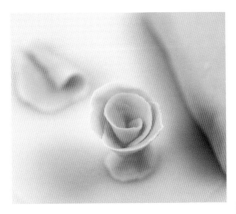

2 Cut out 3–4 small circles using a round cookie cutter. Roll up the first to form the centre, then add the other petals working around the central petal. Keep the petals open at the top so they start to resemble an unfurling bud.

3 Allow flowers to dry and stick in place with a small blob of icing.

Rolling sugarpaste shapes

Some shapes can be rolled out of sugarpaste by hand. This creates an effective 3D shape, but can take some practice to get right!

1 Colour sugarpaste as required. Instead of rolling flat, it can be rolled into simple shapes, like these cherries.

2 Attach to cakes with a little icing.

Attaching sugarpaste shapes

These decorations work best when used on cupcakes with iced, flat tops.

Use a small amount of royal icing in a piping bag to attach sugarpaste shapes to the tops of cakes. Alternatively, brush a little egg white on to shapes to help them stick.

WORKING WITH MARZIPAN

Redolent of medieval feasts, marzipan is a luxurious confection made from ground almonds and fine sugar and is used for covering cakes and making sweets, often coloured and shaped into little fruits, flowers and animals. It can be flavoured with rose or orange flower water.

Marzipan can be used in the same way as sugarpaste to decorate cakes. Tint it, emboss it and roll it into different shapes, using cutters, stamps or templates.

Making marzipan leaves

Small leaves made from rolled-out marzipan can make stunning cake decorations, used by themselves or combined with crystallized or sugarpaste flowers. Try green holly leaves on Christmas cupcakes, or these autumnal oak leaves.

MAKES 8–10 LEAVES
50g/2oz marzipan, tinted as desired
icing (confectioners') sugar, for dusting

1 Roll out the marzipan thinly. Cut out leaves with a cutter, or cut round a card template using a craft knife. Leave to dry on baking parchment.

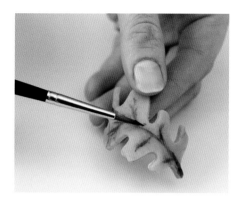

2 For curled leaves, drape the shapes over a rolling pin and leave to dry at room temperature for 2 days. Paint the veins and edges with food colouring using a fine artist's brush.

Mouse in the house

Uncoloured natural marzipan, made with egg whites, works best for marzipan shapes that you want to colour because it accepts colour readily.

MAKES 2
50g/2oz marzipan tinted as desired
small quantity royal icing

1 Take a 2.5cm/1in ball of coloured marzipan and roll it so that it is smooth. Hold the ball between the palms of both hands and gently put pressure on one end to form a cone shape.

2 Make ears from balls of marzipan. Use a modelling tool to indent.

3 Stick on ears with water. Make a round black nose. Create indents for the eyes and fill with icing. Add black eyeballs. Paint on the eyebrows with food colouring. Model a black tail.

4 Place the mice and the black tails on to the tops of cupcakes, just after they have been iced.

Spider in the web

It is difficult to tint marzipan black without changing its consistency, so for an intense shade buy it ready coloured. These creepy crawly marzipan spiders would make great decorations for children's party cakes at Halloween.

MAKES 2
50g/2oz black marzipan
small quantity icing
sprinkles

1 To make the web, cover the top of a cupcake with white glacé icing. Pipe black circles with a fine plain nozzle on top.

2 Starting at the centre and working to the edge, drag a cocktail stick (toothpick) through the lines of icing. Allow to set.

3 Form a smooth round head and a larger round body from marzipan using two balls of black marzipan.

4 Dampen one side of one ball with water and stick the two balls together. Make two indentations for the eyes.

5 Roll eight legs and stick under the body using water. Pipe white eyes in the sockets and a smiley mouth. Add black marzipan eyeballs, and sprinkles on the back.

6 Place the spider on to the web.

Piped decorations
For a simple finish, pipe lines of icing directly on to the surface of the cake. You can also use melted chocolate.

WORKING WITH CHOCOLATE

Everyone likes chocolate, and it is a rewarding and versatile decorating medium for cakes. It can be used to flavour toppings and fillings, or turned into different shapes. For an interesting effect, try using white and dark chocolate marbled together.

Making chocolate cut-outs

You can make abstract shapes, or circles, squares and diamonds, by cutting them out freehand with a sharp knife. If you do not feel confident about cutting chocolate shapes freehand, use cutters.

1 Cover a baking sheet with baking parchment and tape down at each corner. Melt 115g/4oz dark, milk or white chocolate. Pour the chocolate on to the baking parchment.

2 Spread the chocolate over the baking parchment in an even layer with a palette knife. Allow it to stand until the surface of the chocolate is firm enough to cut, but not so hard that it will break. It should no longer feel sticky when touched lightly with your finger.

3 Press the cutter firmly through the chocolate and lift off the paper with a palette knife. Do not touch the surface of the chocolate, or you will leave marks on it.

4 The shapes can be left plain or piped with a contrasting chocolate.

5 Abstract shapes can be cut with a knife, freehand. These are very quick to make but are effective decorations.

Making chocolate leaves

These delicate leaves make a spectacular decoration. Rose leaves are an ideal shape and size, and the prominent veins on their undersides leave a perfect impression in the chocolate. Use a brush to apply the chocolate as evenly as possible.

1 Break a slab of chocolate into small pieces. Put in a heatproof bowl and melt over a pan of simmering water.

2 Brush the chocolate evenly over the underside of clean, dry rose leaves. Put the leaves on a baking sheet lined with baking parchment.

3 Leave in a cool place until the chocolate has set. Peel off each leaf and chill the chocolate leaves in an airtight container until needed.

WORKING WITH FLOWERS

Popular edible flowers include primroses, violets, cowslips, alpine pinks and roses. Try bright blue anchusa, starry-petalled borage or vivid-red pineapple sage. Use them individually or try different combinations.

Crystallizing flowers

This traditional method of preserving summer flowers is simple to do and makes charming and very effective decorations for delicately iced cupcakes. The results can be spectacular, with prettily faded colours and the lingering perfumes of summer. Some flowers, such as primroses, cowslips, borage, sage and anchusa, are easy to pull away from their green calyx and can be crystallized whole. Daisies, roses and pinks are often best divided into individual petals, although you might consider treating entire small flowerheads for a real showpiece. Fresh crystallized flowers that retain their moisture need using quickly, but flowers that are dried thoroughly in a warm place for 24–36 hours prior to crystallizing will last for a few months.

selection of petals and/or flowers
1 egg white
50g/2oz/¼ cup caster (superfine) sugar

1 Gather flowers when they are dry, and select clean, perfect specimens. Trim and prepare individual petals or whole flowers. Beat the egg white lightly and put it and the sugar in separate saucers.

2 Pick up each petal or flower and paint the entire surface, front and back, carefully with the egg white, using an artist's brush.

3 Dredge on both sides with caster sugar so that it sticks to the egg white and coats the flower or petal.

4 Lay the flowers and petals on baking parchment and leave them in a warm, dry place until completely dry and crisp. Store them in a sealed container.

Raw eggs
These should not be eaten by pregnant women, babies, young children or the elderly. If in doubt, use powdered egg white for coating the flowers. It will work just as well.

MAKING MARSHMALLOWS
This sweet confection, with its soft texture, is perfect for topping muffins for children.

MAKES 98 TINY MARSHMALLOWS
50g/2oz/¹⁄₂ cup icing (confectioners')
sugar, sifted
50g/2oz/¹⁄₂ cup cornflour
(cornstarch), sifted
225g/8oz/generous 1 cup sugar
15ml/1 tbsp glucose syrup
9 sheets leaf gelatine
5ml/1 tsp vanilla extract
2 egg whites

1 Lightly oil a shallow baking tin (pan) 30 x 20 x 2.5cm (12 x 8 x 1in). Dust it with half of the icing sugar and cornflour, sifted together, to evenly coat the base.

2 Place the sugar, glucose syrup and 200ml/7fl oz/scant 1 cup water in a pan and bring slowly to the boil, stirring frequently until the sugar dissolves. Boil rapidly until the temperature reaches 127°C/260°F.

3 Soak the leaf gelatine in 150ml/¹⁄₄ pint/²⁄₃ cup cold water and set aside for 10 minutes.

4 Melt the gelatine, in a pan, in its soaking water over a low heat. Pour the leaf gelatine liquid into the sugar syrup. Stir twice. Pour into a metal bowl. Stir in the vanilla.

5 Place the egg whites in a bowl and whisk into stiff peaks. Continue whisking and pour in the syrup in a slow, thin stream. It will gradually start to thicken to the stiff peak stage. When all the syrup is added continue to beat for 10 minutes until thick and glossy.

6 Pour into the prepared tin and smooth the surface with a wet knife. Chill for 1 hour.

7 Cut into squares and dust with the remaining icing sugar and cornflour mixture. Use to top iced muffins or store in an airtight container.

Packaging and presentation

Have fun packaging and gift wrapping your favourite cakes. A single beautifully boxed cupcake makes a charming small gift for a friend, or you could pack a whole batch to give as favours at the end of a party. Muffins and cupcakes in decorated cups made from paper look lovely on a celebration table.

As you are making your cupcakes or muffins, think about their final presentation. Use different-shaped muffin tins (pans), taller dariole moulds, or even mini terracotta plant pots or

ABOVE: *An attractive stand will make your cakes look their absolute best.*

ABOVE: *Simple cakes dusted with icing sugar may suit formal occasions.*

ovenproof coffee cups. There are many different styles of paper cases available, or, for a change, use elegant squares of baking parchment to line your tin.

Displaying accessories

Paper cases, which are available in a wonderful assortment of colours and many patterns – flowery, stripy, dotty, with little red hearts or with fluffy chicks – are far too pretty to be hidden away in the back of a kitchen cupboard or drawer. Store them in a large glass jar; there are so many attractively decorated ones to choose from. Don't forget the other cake accessories you might have collected: silver dragées, sugarpaste decorations, and coloured ribbons for gift wrapping your freshly baked creations. These, too, will look equally attractive presented in glass jars to decorate your kitchen. The sight of this ever-ready supply of baking accessories and cake decorations may even inspire you to bake more beautiful cakes more often for family and friends.

ABOVE: *Use multi-coloured decorations for children's cupcakes and muffins.*

Serving your cakes

If you are going to be serving your cupcakes or muffins to other people – whether at a casual coffee morning with friends, a children's party or a more lavish occasion like a wedding – it is important to take the time to think about the presentation.

Once you have chosen your recipe, try to match the decoration of your cakes to the occasion. Children will love brightly coloured toppings and haphazard decorations, while muted, subtle colours and a more uniform approach may be appropriate for a formal occasion. Choose pretty plates and cake stands that will show off all the hard work you have put into your baking and make your cakes look as good as they taste!

Patterned card cake cups

It can be fun to personalize your fresh muffins and cupcakes with attractive home-made paper cups that wrap around the paper case. Simply slot the cakes inside before you serve them. You will need some coloured strips of decorative craft paper (or wallpaper that has the right thickness and flexibility), a selection of decorative standard weight papers, decorative craft paper and thin coloured ribbons.

Cut strips of craft paper 3–4cm/ 1¼–1½in wide and long enough to fit round the circumference of the cupcakes. Bend the strip into a circle and stick the ends together with small strips of sticky tape to make the cake cup. Make sure it is just large enough to sit the cakes or muffins inside: you should still see a tiny margin of the frilly paper case above the top of the card, so make a trial one before cutting out all the strips. Cut a second, slightly narrower strip from

ABOVE: *Fit two cupcakes in a larger box to make an indulgent present for two.*

decorative craft paper or coloured papers and stick it in place along the centre of the card strip.

Finally, tie a length of thin coloured cord or ribbon around the waist of the paper cup, finishing with a bow at the front (with the join at the back). Alternatively, you can add small paper decorations: butterflies for summer cakes, rabbits for Easter, numbers for special birthdays, and white doves for wedding cupcakes make appropriate motifs for different occasions.

Presentation boxes

For birthday party gifts and holiday treats, display scrumptious cakes inside small clear plastic boxes. Add a gorgeous ribbon and a paper blossom to make your edible gifts more special. Plain card gift boxes in pretty colours turn a beautifully iced cupcake into a lovely gift. Choose colours and styles to suit your cakes (or choose the wrappings

ABOVE: *A box of mini-muffins makes an excellent gift for a birthday tea party.*

first and colour the icing and decorations to match your presentation theme). Line the box lavishly with tissue to keep your creations safe inside, and tie up the parcel with a length of satin ribbon and a pretty tag.

Presentation tip

Remember to match the paper cake cases to the occasion for a special occasion: silver for a silver wedding, red for a ruby wedding and so on.

ABOVE: *A host of ready-cut paper motifs are available from craft suppliers.*

Index